Aprie Prichard.

D1626623

THE FIRSTBORN

CHRISTOPHER FRY

THE FIRSTBORN

A Play in Three Acts

Second Edition

Geoffrey Cumberlege

OXFORD UNIVERSITY PRESS

LONDON NEW YORK TORONTO

Oxford University Press, Amen House, London, E.C. 4
GLASGOW NEW YORK TORONTO MELBOURNE WELLINGTON
BOMBAY CALCUTTA MADRAS CAPE TOWN
Geoffrey Cumberlege, Publisher to the University

First Published by the
Cambridge University Press 1946
Reissued by the
Oxford University Press 1949
and reprinted in 1950 *(twice) and* 1951
Second Edition (revised) February 1952; *reprinted in July* 1952

PRINTED IN GREAT BRITAIN

To

MY MOTHER

and

MY BROTHER

FOREWORD

THIS play—begun as long ago as 1938, though not finished until 1945 after four years when circumstance made me neglect it—has a title which at first may seem to quarrel with most of the action, since the chief protagonist is Moses. But I hope, after a little acquaintance, the figure of life which Ramases presents will be seen to take a central place from his first entrance to the end. The character of Moses is a movement towards maturity, towards a balancing of life within the mystery, where the conflicts and dilemmas are the trembling of the balance. In the last scene he suffers a momentary spiritual death ('I followed a light into a blindness') at the moment when the firstborn's physical death creates the Hebrews' freedom; and his resurrection from that, to become the great leader, though only hinted at as the curtain falls, carries with it something of the life of Ramases.

> Death was their question to us, and our lives
> Become their understanding or perplexity.
> And by living to answer them, we also answer
> Our own impermanence.

Ramases lives a boyhood almost identical with Moses' own; he and the Hebrew Shendi between them draw the frontiers of combat altogether differently from the lines laid down by accepted human action. Ramases is the innocence, humanity, vigour, and worth which stand on the enemy side, not altering the justice or necessity of Moses' cause, but linking the ways of men and the ways of God with a deep and urgent question-mark.

I made certain alterations and cuts immediately after the Edinburgh Festival production in 1948; and for this edition I have revised those alterations, refashioned the last scene, and cut further.

This is a welcome opportunity to say how much I was helped, in the play's early stages, by the encouragement of Gerard Hopkins and the late Charles Williams; and by Frank Kendon, of the Cambridge University Press, whose belief in it, in 1946, first saw it into print.

C. F.

28 *December* 1951

CONTENTS

ACT ONE

ACT TWO

ACT THREE

THE FIRSTBORN

Gateway Theatre, Edinburgh, 6 *September* 1948

Anath Bithiah	ATHENE SEYLER
Teusret	DEIDRE DOONE
Seti the Second	ROBERT SPEAIGHT
Ramases	PAUL HANSARD
Moses	IVAN BRANDT
Aaron	ROBERT SANSOM
Miriam	HENZIE RAEBURN
Shendi	ROBERT RIETTY

Directed by E. Martin Browne

Winter Garden Theatre, London, 29 *January* 1952

Anath Bithiah	BARBARA EVEREST
Teusret	RUTH TROUNCER
Seti the Second	MARK DIGNAM
Ramases	TONY BRITTON
Moses	ALEC CLUNES
Aaron	CYRIL LUCKHAM
Miriam	DOROTHY REYNOLDS
Shendi	ROBERT RIETTY

Directed by John Fernald

CHARACTERS

ANATH BITHIAH, *Pharaoh's sister*
TEUSRET, *Pharaoh's daughter*
SETI THE SECOND, *the Pharaoh*
RAMASES, *his son*
MOSES
AARON, *his brother*
MIRIAM, *his sister*
SHENDI, *Miriam's son*
Two overseers, a Minister (KEF)
A guard and a servant

*The action of the play takes place in
the summer of 1200 B.C., alternating
between Pharaoh's palace and
Miriam's tent*

ACT ONE

SCENE ONE

The terrace of the palace of Seti the Second, at Tanis. A morning in the summer of 1200 B.C. *A flight of steps (unseen) leads down through a gate to open ground. The terrace looks out upon an incompleted pyramid.*

A scream.

Enter from the palace ANATH BITHIAH, *a woman of fifty, sister to the Pharaoh, and* TEUSRET, *a girl of fifteen, the Pharaoh's daughter*

ANATH. What was it, Teusret?

TEUSRET.   Did you hear it too?

ANATH. Some man is dead. That scream was password to a grave.
   Look there: up go the birds!

TEUSRET.   The heat on this terrace!
   You could bake on these stones, Aunt Anath.

ANATH.   Ask who it was.

TEUSRET. They're working steadily at father's tomb.
   There's no sign of trouble.

ANATH.   We're too far off to see.
   We should know more if we could see their faces.

TEUSRET [*calling down the steps*]. Guard! Come up here.

ANATH.   I should like to be certain.
   Oh, that pyramid! Everyday, watching it build,
   Will make an old woman of me early.
   It will cast a pretty shadow when it's done.
   Two hundred more men were taken on today,
   Did you know that, Teusret? You father's in a hurry.

Their sweat would be invaluable to the farmers in this drought.
What pains they take to house a family of dust.

TEUSRET. It's a lovely tomb.

ANATH.   Yes, so it may be.
But what shall we do with all that air to breathe
And no more breath? I could as happily lie
And wait for eternal life in something smaller.

Enter A GUARD

TEUSRET. What was that scream we heard?

GUARD.   It's nothing, madam.

ANATH. You are right. Nothing. It was something once
But now it is only a scare of birds in the air
And a pair of women with their nerves uncovered;
Nothing.

TEUSRET. Who was it screamed?

GUARD.   One of the builders
Missed his footing, madam; merely an Israelite.
They're digging him into the sand. No, over to the left.

TEUSRET. Oh yes, I see them now.—That was all I wanted.

[*Exit* THE GUARD

So that's all right.

ANATH.   Can you remember your cousin?

TEUSRET. Why, which cousin?

ANATH.   My foster son. You knew him
When you were little. He lived with us in the palace.

TEUSRET. The birds are back on the roof now.

ANATH.   Moses, Teusret.

[2]

TEUSRET. What, Aunt? Yes, I think I remember. I remember
A tall uncle. Was he only a cousin?
He used to drum his helmet with a dagger
While he sang us regimental marches to get us to sleep.
It never did. Why?

ANATH.   No reason. I thought of him.
Well, they've buried the man in the sand. We'd better
Find our morning again and use what's left.

TEUSRET. Why did you think of him? Why *then* particularly?

ANATH. Why not then? Sometimes he blows about my brain
Like litter at the end of a public holiday.
I have obstinate affections. Ask your father.
He would tell you, if it wasn't impolitic
To mention Moses, what a girl of fire
I was, before I made these embers.
He could tell you how I crossed your grandfather,
And your grandfather was a dynasty in himself.
Oh Teusret, what a day of legend that was!
I held forbidden Israel in my arms
And growled on my stubborn doorstep, till I had my way.

TEUSRET. What do you mean?

ANATH.   Well, never mind.

TEUSRET.   I do.
You've told me so far.

ANATH.   Keep it to yourself then.
The summer of '24 had brilliant days
And unprecedented storms. The striped linen
You once cut up for a doll's dress was the dress
Made for me that summer. It was the summer
When my father, your grandfather, published the pronounce-
    ment.

[3]

TEUSRET. What pronouncement?

ANATH.   That all the boys of Jewdom
Should be killed. Not out of spite, Teusret; necessity.
Your grandfather ordered that Defence of the Realm be painted
At the head of the document, in azure and silver.
It made it easier for him.

TEUSRET.   Were they killed?

ANATH. Yes, they all died of a signature. Or we thought so,
Until the thirtieth of August. I went bathing on that day.
I was a girl then, Teusret, and played with the Nile
As though with a sister. And afterwards as I waded
To land again, pushing the river with my knees,
The wash rocked a little ark out
Into the daylight: and in the ark I found
A tiny weeping Israel who had failed
To be exterminated. When I stooped
With my hair dripping on to his face
He stopped in a screwed-up wail and looked.
And when I found my hands and crowded him
Into my breast, he buried like a burr.
And when I spoke I laughed, and when I laughed
I cried, he was so enchanting. I was ready
To raise a hornet's nest to keep him; in fact
I raised one. All the court flew up and buzzed.
But what could they do? Not even my Pharaoh-father
Could sting him out of my arms. So he grew up
Into your tall cousin, Egyptian
From beard to boots and, what was almost better,
A soldier of genius. You don't remember
How I held you on this terrace, to see him come home from war?
It was ten years ago. Do you remember

[4]

The shrieking music, and half Egypt shouting
Conqueror! Peacemaker!

TEUSRET.   No.

ANATH.   They have all tried to forget.
They have blotted him out of the records, but not out
Of my memory.

TEUSRET.   Why did they blot him out?

ANATH. I might have known that I should say too much.

TEUSRET. Aunt, you must tell me.

ANATH.   Well, no doubt I meant to.
The day I held you here, he came as the conqueror
Of Abyssinia. In all the windows and doors
Women elbowed and cracked their voices; and men
Hung on the gates and the trees; and children sang
The usual songs, conducted by their teachers.

TEUSRET. Yes, but what happened to make him——

ANATH. All right, I'm coming to it, Teusret. The day after,
For the country-side also to be able to see the hero,
He went to inspect the city being built at Pithom.—
My book was closed from that day forward.
He went round with an officer who unfortunately
Was zealous but unintelligent. Silly man:
Silly, silly man. He found a labourer
Idling or resting, and he thought, I suppose,
'I'll show this prince that I'm worth my position'
And beat the workman. A Jewish bricklayer.
He beat him senseless.

TEUSRET.   And then?

ANATH. Moses turned—turned to what was going on—
Turned himself and his world turtle. It was
As though an inward knife scraped his eyes clean.

[5]

The General of Egypt, the Lion and the Prince
Recognized his mother's face in the battered body
Of a bricklayer; saw it was not the face above
His nursery, not my face after all.
He knew his seed. And where my voice had hung till then
Now voices descending from ancestral Abraham
Congregated on him. And he killed
His Egyptian self in the self of that Egyptian
And buried that self in the sand.

TEUSRET.   Aunt—

Enter A GUARD

GUARD.   The Pharaoh.
Madam, the Pharaoh is here.

ANATH.   Can we look innocent?

Enter SETI. *Exit* THE GUARD

TEUSRET. Good morning, father.

SETI.   Go indoors, my Teusret.

                                [*Exit* TEUSRET

Where is Moses?

ANATH. Seti!

SETI.   Where is Moses? You will know.
In what country? Doing what?

ANATH.   Why Moses?

SETI. I need him.

ANATH.   I've no reason to remember.
I'm without him.

SETI.   But you know.

[6]

ANATH.   Why should I know?
   Why should I? When the sun goes down do I have to know
   Where and how it grovels under the world?
   I thought he was a dust-storm we had shut outside.
   Even now I sometimes bite on the grit.

SETI. I have found him necessary.
   Libya is armed along the length of her frontier,
   And the South's like sand, shifting and uncertain.
   I need Moses.—We have discarded in him
   A general of excellent perception.

ANATH. He's discarded, rightly or wrongly. We've let him go.

SETI. Deeds lie down at last, and so did his.
   Out in the wilderness, after two days' flight,
   His deed lay down, knowing what it had lost him.
   Under the boredom of thorn-trees his deed cried out
   For Egypt and died. Ten years long he has lugged
   This dead thing after him. His loyalty needn't be questioned.

ANATH. We're coming to something strange when a normal day
   Opens and lets in the past. He may remember
   Egypt. He's in Midian.

SETI.   In what part of Midian?

ANATH. Wherever buckets are fetched up out of wells
   Or in his grave.

SETI.   We'll find him. If we have to comb
   Midian to its shadows we'll find him.

ANATH.   He's better where he is.

SETI. He is essential to my plans.

ANATH.   I tell you
   He is better where he is. For you or me
   He's better where he is.

[7]

We have seen different days without him
And I have done my hair a different way.
Leave him alone to bite his lips.

> [*His eye is caught by something below and beyond the terrace*

SETI.   What's this,
What is this crowd?

ANATH.   It's Ramases! No qualms
For the dynasty, with a son as popular as he is.

SETI. There's half the city round him. Where are his guards?

ANATH. There: a little behind.

SETI.   The boy's too careless.
I'm not altogether at rest in the way he's growing,
His good graces for no-matter-whom.
He must learn to let the needs of Egypt rule him.

ANATH. He will learn. He is learning.

SETI.   Egypt should pray so.

ANATH. I would hazard a guess that Egypt's women
Have prayed for him often enough. Ra, raising
An eyebrow stiff with the concentration of creation
Probably says: That boy again? We'd better
Make something of him early and have them satisfied.
O, Ramases will be all right.

SETI.   I hope,
I hope.

> *Enter* RAMASES, *a boy of eighteen*

RAMASES. Did you see the excitement? I think it's the drought.
Like the air, we're all quivering with heat.
Do you find that, Aunt? Either you must sleep like the dead
Or something violent must happen.

ANATH.   Look: your father.

[8]

RAMASES. I didn't see you, father. I'm sorry, sir.
Did I interrupt state matters?

SETI.   What morning have you had?

RAMASES. Holiday—books rolled up, military exercises
Over, and no social engagements. I've been fowling
Down at the marshes.

ANATH.   Any luck?

RAMASES.   Not much flesh
But a paradise of feathers. I was out before daybreak.

ANATH. It's a good marksman who hunts by batlight.

RAMASES.   But I
Waited for daylight. Until then the marsh was a torpor.
I clucked and clapped as the sun rose
And up shot so much whistle and whirr
I could only hold my spear and laugh.
All the indignant wings of the marshes
Flocking to the banner of Tuesday
To avoid the Prince of Egypt!
Off they flapped into the mist
Looking about for Monday
The day they had lived in peace: and finding nothing
Back they wheeled to Tuesday.
I had recovered myself by then and killed
One that had the breast of a chestnut.
At last he could feel the uninterrupted darkness
Of an addled egg. I watched his nerves flinching
As they felt how dark that darkness was.
I found myself trying to peer into his death.
It seemed a long way down. The morning and it
Were oddly separate,
Though the bird lay in the sun: separate somehow
Even from contemplation.

[9]

ANATH. Excellent spirits
To make a success of a holiday.

RAMASES. Only for a moment.

SETI. This afternoon I have business for you.   [*He turns to go in*

RAMASES. Very well.

SETI. Was that thunder?

ANATH. They're dumping new stone for the
pyramid.

RAMASES. Two men came through the marshes before I left;
Jews, but not our Jews: or one of them
Was not; he seemed a man of prosperity
Although some miles of sun and dust were on him.

SETI. Aliens?

RAMASES. Yes; but one of them I felt
I should have known. How could I?
I passed them again as I came home. They stood
To watch the crowd. I looked across and smiled
But got no smiles from them. And one, the tall one——

ANATH. Very tall?

RAMASES. Yes, he was tall. It was he
Who is somehow in my memory.

ANATH. Seti——

SETI. Well?

ANATH. Is it possible that someone hasn't waited to be recalled?
Is it possible?

SETI. It is not possible.

ANATH. Your thoughts are leaning that way too.
Sometimes the unaccountable stalks in.

SETI. Which way were they travelling, Ramases?

RAMASES. This way. If I had only thought of them sooner
We could have seen them go by.—Sir!
They are standing here at the foot of the stairway. How long
Can they have been there? Shall I speak to them?

ANATH. He has stood all day under my brain's stairway.
Seti, who is there? Which foremost, Ramases?
The tall one?

RAMASES.　　　　　Yes. Who's in your mind?

ANATH.　　　　　　　　　　　The tall one.
The tall one.

　　　　　　　　　　　[RAMASES *goes down the steps*

　　　　　So he is back; and small-talk
Has to block a draught up ten years old.

SETI. Why has he come?

ANATH.　　　　　You said he longed for Egypt.

SETI. I think so.

ANATH.　　　　But what am I in Egypt?
A dead king's daughter.

　　　Re-enter RAMASES, *followed by* MOSES *and* AARON

SETI.　　　　　　　　What words can I find to fit
So ghostly a homecoming? Understand you are welcome.
Whatever uncertainty you have can go.
We welcome you. Look who is here.

ANATH. He has seen me. We have looked at one another.

SETI. We'll absolve ourselves of the ten years. Who is this?

MOSES. My brother.

SETI.　　　　　　I had not heard you had a brother.

[11]

ANATH. A brother, a sister—and a mother. All the three.

SETI. I told my sister we must have you back.
And so we must, and so Egypt must; and it seems
That we have. You are come promptly at the word, Moses.

MOSES. This is not why I came.

SETI.   You would scarcely foresee it.

MOSES. I am not who you think. I am a stranger.

SETI. Not by a vein or a hair. The past is forgotten.
You are a prince of Egypt.

MOSES.   The prince of Egypt
Died the day he fled.

SETI.   What do you mean?

MOSES. That prince of Egypt died. I am the Hebrew
Smitten out of the shadow of that prince,
Vomited out of his dry lips, the cry
Whipped off the sanded tongue of that prince of Egypt.

SETI. What has this long discomfort done for you,
My friend? It has made you bitter.

MOSES.   Make no mistake;
I have done very well for myself. I haven't come to beg.
Why was it you decided to ask me to come back?

SETI. Isn't it time we laid the crippling ghost
That haunts us? You evidently thought so too
To come so far.

MOSES.   You've a better reason that that.

SETI. Why should you want reasons when you have come
On your own initiative? Why are you here?
I am asking you candidly. Why did you come?

MOSES. My blood heard my blood weeping
Far off like the swimming of fear under the sea,
The sobbing at night below the garden. I heard
My blood weeping. It is here it wept and weeps.
It was from here I heard coming this drum of despair,
Under your shoes, under your smile, and under
The foundations of your tomb. From Egypt.

ANATH. What was it, Seti, that lay down and died?

SETI. Why are you here?

MOSES.   To be close to this
That up to now has only made me uneasy,
As though a threat of evil whispered beyond
Control under the wind. I could be
Uneasy and still eat in Midian.
I could be Pharaoh in Midian, but in Egypt
I knew I should be Moses.

SETI.   Still you haven't
Answered my question. Come, what do you want?

MOSES. First, that you should know what you are doing.

SETI. Take care, Moses.

ANATH.   And secondly?

MOSES.   What can I hope
From that until he has understood the first?

SETI. What is this mood you have come in which is so ready
To abuse a decent welcome? There is something shipwreck
About you that will not do for peaceful places.
Steady yourself if we're to understand one another.
I am the Pharaoh, Moses, not the young uncle
Of the Heliopolis classroom, nor your messroom brother.

[13]

MOSES. A man has more to be than a Pharaoh.
He must dare to outgrow the security
Of partial blindness. I'm not speaking now
To your crown; I'm speaking to your merciless mischief.

SETI. You have coarsened during your exile. What you say
Hasn't even the virtue of clarity. If you wish
To consider my offer of reinstatement, go
And consider. I can be patient. Egypt can do
Her work on you like a generous woman, given
Her time.   [*He glances at* ANATH
        Midian will wash off in the Nile.
Go on, go on, I shall not remember this morning.

MOSES. I think you will. My brother has lived these days
In amongst Israel, while I was sleeping.
He knows both the truth and the injury better than I can.
Let him speak what he knows.

AARON. Twelve hundred thousand Israelites are under
Your dominion. Of these two hundred and twenty thousand
Only, are men. The rest are in the proportion
Of four hundred and fifty thousand women
And five hundred and thirty thousand children.

SETI. I have my census-takers.

AARON.   So perhaps
Has Death got his; but I think he has not referred
His undertakings to your dynastic understanding.
Here I have his estimate: between April and July
Six hundred and one deaths suffered in old age
But an old age of forced labour, their backs bent twice,
Under the weight of years and under the mule-whip.
Also thirty-eight deaths of healthy men
Who made some show of reluctance or momentary
Impatience.

[14]

MOSES.   That was a good cure. They are now
    Patient for all eternity.

AARON.   Also the deaths
    Of a hundred pregnant women, forced to dig
    Until they had become their own gravediggers.
    Also the deaths of eighty-four children, twelve
    Unofficial crucifixions . . .

SETI.   This is intolerable
    Singsong! Am I to compose the epitaphs
    For every individual grave of this trying summer?
    I have my figures. I do not need yours.
    I have put men to a purpose who otherwise
    Would have had not the least meaning.

MOSES. Not the least meaning, except the meaning
    Of the breath in your lungs, the mystery of existing
    At all. What have we approached or conceived
    When we have conquered and built a world? Even
    Though civilization became perfect? What then?
    We have only put a crown on the skeleton.
    It is the individual man
    In his individual freedom who can mature
    With his warm spirit the unripe world.
    They are your likeness, these men, even to nightmares.
    I have business with Egypt, one more victory for her,
    A better one than Ethiopia:
    That she should come to see her own shame
    And discover justice for my people.

SETI. You have fermented in your Midian bottle.
    But lately I have learnt an obstinate patience.
    We should have done better to have met
    Out of the sun. We can do better than this
    And so we shall yet, later, at a cooler time.

[15]

Where will you sleep? We will see you have food.
Do you remember, I wonder, the palace nectarine?
I said, where will you lodge?

MOSES.   With my sister, Miriam.

SETI [*to* ANATH]. Do you know where that is?

ANATH.   Perfectly.

SETI [*going in*].   Very well.

ANATH. Now he will not sleep again tonight.

MOSES. I hope that none of us will sleep again
Until we all can sleep.

ANATH.   And so once more
We see each other. You have chosen a fine day.

       [MOSES *waits.* ANATH *says no more. He goes with* AARON

ANATH. I taught him to walk, Ramases. I also taught him
To speak and say his alphabet. I taught you your
Alphabet also; and also Teusret hers.
I have been a really useful woman.

RAMASES.   Where
Does his sister live?

ANATH.   Why do you want to know?

RAMASES. I wondered where it might be.

ANATH.   She has a tent
By the brick-kiln.

RAMASES.   I liked that man.

ANATH. So have others before you. Like him, Ramases,
Forget him, and let us live in peace.

RAMASES. I shall go and find him.

ANATH. Ramases, I ask you to forget him.

[16]

RAMASES.   How?

ANATH. What would make it difficult?

RAMASES.   Can you forget him?

ANATH. He has gone.

RAMASES.   And something of us, I think, went with him.

ANATH. Well, you will let him go. I have asked you.

RAMASES.   No.
  I love you, you know that. But trust me a little.
  I shall be discreet.   [*Exit* RAMASES

ANATH.   Ramases!—No,
  What should I be doing, turning his feet
  Towards my fears?   [*She goes to the parapet*

                   Enter TEUSRET

TEUSRET. Aunt Anath—

ANATH.   Do you remember, Teusret?
  A man fell from the pyramid—only this morning.

                      CURTAIN

                   SCENE TWO

MIRIAM'S *tent*.   MOSES [*in the entrance*].   MIRIAM.

MOSES. Miriam! Miriam!

MIRIAM.   Is it my brother? Yes;
  You have his immovable look. Aaron told me
  To expect you.

MOSES.   Can you be Miriam?

C   [17]

MIRIAM.   A kind
    Of residue. Sit down, if you don't mind.
    I dislike answering questions. Ask me nothing.
    I am very well; I have nothing to offer you
    To drink.

MOSES.   I'm glad to be with you after so long.

MIRIAM. You will find it very tiresome after five or six minutes.
    I repeat myself unendurably, like the Creation.
    Your only hope is to deaden yourself to me
    And it.

AARON [*in the entrance*]. Your name runs like fire, like an ostrich!
    You didn't wait to hear, but the sergeant at the gate
    Is full of it. They've started campaigns of gossip
    And altercation in the assembly-gardens—
    As soon as this; before you've even been seen!

MOSES. And what will this do for us?

AARON.   Surely it suggests
    They're taking sides? It was noticed a minister's wife
    Was wearing an M in small lilies; her daughter snatched them off
    And threw them among the pigeons. How can Seti
    Assure himself what size your faction is?
    Egypt loves and hates you inextricably.

MOSES. Egypt is afraid. Love me? No;
    They're afraid to be without me.

AARON. That will pass for love.

MOSES. They love me from the bottom of their greed.
    Give me the bad news. What men have we lost?

MIRIAM. So you're not only here on a visit to your sister.

AARON. Here is a list. It's not complete.

[18]

MIRIAM.   I've had
  Enough of trouble.

MOSES.   Rahnor, Janeth, Pathrusim—
  Is he lost? Pathrusim? The sand of Egypt
  Is abominably the richer.—Hadoram, Seth,
  Havilah, Dodanim . . .

MIRIAM.   Why do you read
  Dead men's names? There are some of us still breathing.
  Your sister, for example, is still alive,
  Figuratively speaking. I imagined
  You would have plenty to tell me. Have you not?
  Am I always to know nothing of you?

MOSES.   These names are what I am.

MIRIAM. They are yesterday's life. I liked many of them very well;
  But we no longer have anything in common.

AARON. Are we to forget them because we have lost them?

MIRIAM.   To wish
  To be with them comes too easily.

MOSES.   This tent
  Is stifling.

MIRIAM. I keep it closed. I have no liking
  For what goes on outside.

MOSES.   When do they say
  The mountains last had rain?

MIRIAM.   Nine months ago.

MOSES. It's time for parturition.
  Look: what you shut out is a withering city.
  City of Egypt. This land once I worshipped,
  And now I cannot be sure what I bring against her
  In my heart. This noon, like every other noon,

[19]

Still groans with the laborious wheels which drew
The Nile water. There is little difference
Between ourselves and those blindfolded oxen.
We also do the thing we cannot see,
Hearing the creaking pivot and only knowing
That we labour.

MIRIAM.   Why did you bring him? Take yourselves off!
This is my tent, and it's not for restless hands.
He's a dangermaker still. Only watch his hands!

AARON. What has he said, Miriam?

MIRIAM.   I have a son
And that is all I rest on. There's a man
Who should have been my brother. A king's daughter
Swallowed him and spat out this outlaw. I'll
Not have any more in the family.

AARON.   What should make them?

MIRIAM. You and he. I know. Two years ago
I had it all: the surly men coming in here,
One at a time by signal, hardly nodding
Towards me, covering the table with their knife-cuts
To show how revolution must come, and freedom,
And idiocy; till a beetle striking the lamp
Or the coal settling, would shiver through us all
As though a dagger had sung into the pole.
And Espah and Zoad are dead from it. And you
In a night of loud hyenas went over the border.
Not again. I'll keep my nights of sleep, and I'll keep
My son.

AARON.   In this country of murder?

MIRIAM.   I'll keep my son
In whatever country.

MOSES. Happily?

MIRIAM. We have
A way of living. We have the habit. Well?
It becomes a kind of pleasantness.

MOSES. You have gone
With the dead after all, but you pretend not to see them.
Miriam, we have to speak to them with our lives.
Death was their question to us, and our lives
Become their understanding or perplexity.
And by living to answer them, we also answer
Our own impermanence. But this rule of Egypt
Denies us life, Miriam, and gives us nothing
With which we can outspeak our graves.

MIRIAM. I am angry;
The pity is I am angry. I must pretend
You have said nothing.

AARON. But do you understand him?
In fact, do I understand him?

MOSES. When I was a child,
Miriam, and you came like comfort to the huge
Nursery of the Pharaohs, we'd go hand
In hand along your stories, Hebrew stories
Which like contraband you put quietly in
To become my nature. What have you for me now?

MIRIAM. How she disliked me then! But what a talent
For condescension she had. I never saw you
After you were a child except by waiting
Among the crowd in the streets. There was no need
To come from Midian to tell me what my life is;
I have a bowing acquaintance with it. I knew it
When I hid you to save you from the knives.

[21]

Before I could talk it talked to me
In most difficult words.

MOSES.   What words, Miriam?

MIRIAM. Pogrom, for one. And the curses of children
When I ran towards them expecting to play.
We have a wildfowl quality of blood,
Moses, temptation for sportsmen.

MOSES.   Go on.

MIRIAM.   With what
If you please? Do you know the secret which will change
Our spoor? Our grandfather was stoned. I imagine
Creation tried our blood, and brought it in guilty.

MOSES. It was the verdict of Chaos.

MIRIAM.   The thick of Chaos
Can still be smelt in the air, then. It was never
Properly resolved.

MOSES.   And I believed
I had strength!

MIRIAM.   Your quarrel is with what things are.

MOSES. Above all, with what I am, the inconsiderable
Life, born of such distances of suffering,
And yet my spirit
Paces the condemned cell, the human body,
Incapable, weaponless, fettered with flesh, drinking
The moisture of the walls. Is the spirit
So masterly, that nature must obstruct it
Or be consumed? I feel it. Oh, it points!
I am there, beyond myself, if I could reach
To where I am. Miriam, you have shown me too much.

MIRIAM. One grows accustomed.

[22]

AARON.   You will find the approach
   And the means you want, I'm confident. Something
   Will soon open a way to action.

RAMASES [*in the tent-opening*].   Uncle.
   I knew you as that. When I have thought of you
   It has been as my uncle. You may not like it.
   You may not want to see me, even.

MOSES. Welcome and unwelcome.

RAMASES.   I haven't come
   From my father. I used schoolboy's worship, like myrrh
   And cassia, with gums of memory,
   To perpetuate you: the immense and affable
   God in general's uniform, who came
   And went between wars, who filled the schoolroom; and I
   Could call him uncle. So when the memory
   Broke its wrappings, and stood speaking like a man
   On a noonday terrace, I decided to come nearer.

MOSES. Come on, then, and send the god to vanish finally
   Into the lie that he always was.

RAMASES.   You spoke
   To my father too suddenly.

MOSES.   Yes, we're precipitous,
   We gods. We threw off the world, vegetable
   And animal too, on the impulse of an imaginative
   Moment. But we lost interest.

RAMASES.   You mean
   I'm a boy to you still.

MOSES.   You came by your boyhood honestly.
   Mine I stole. I had no right to it.

AARON.   Why
    Do you turn him away, Moses? Why not talk to him?

MOSES. What would we talk of, Aaron? What quiet subject?
    They tell me centuries of horror brood
    In this vivid kingdom of fertile mud. Do you think
    If we swung the rattle of conversation
    Those centuries would fly off like so many crows?
    They would wheel above us and come to feed again.

AARON. But what do you think of? I sometimes call you, to myself,
    A gate without a key. You'll open when you will.
    Such a gate must lead somewhere, so I believe,
    Though perhaps that sounds fanciful. Where shall we find a better
    Opportunity?

RAMASES.   I have my father mapped
    So that I know which way to travel. Listen,
    Uncle—he says he would have recalled you, which means
    He needs you here. He'll be friendly if you let him.
    I kept a buckle of your uniform—this one, the lion-head.
    Take it again, take our army and be our general.
    You'll become inseparable from Egypt's safety;
    Then he will listen. Then you can direct
    His goodwill past yourself to these Israelites.

AARON. It's true. You have the buckle, and we're agreed, then.
    My dreams were less; not a third as felicitous.

MOSES. Egypt and Israel both in me together!
    How would that be managed? I should wolf
    Myself to keep myself nourished. I could play
    With wars, oh God, very pleasantly. You know
    I prosper in a cloud of dust—you're wise
    To offer me that. And Egypt would still be,
    In spite of my fathers, a sufficient cause.

[24]

AARON. Yes, it would be sufficient.

MOSES.   Splendid, then.
    What armour shall I wear? What ancestral metal
    Above my heart? Rib, thighbone and skull:
    Bones from the mines of Egypt. I will clank
    To Egypt's victory in Israel's bones.
    Does this please you? Does it not? Admire
    How when preparing a campaign I become
    Oblivious to day and night, and in
    The action, obsessed. How will that do? I make
    My future, put glory into Egypt, enjoy myself
    Into your father's confidence—yes, that,
    I know; and being there, perhaps I coax
    Little concessions for the Hebrew cause
    To justify me.—Idiot, idiot!
    I should have lost them, Aaron, and be lost,
    More than when in Midian I sat
    Over my food and let them trudge in my bowels.

AARON. I have faith in your judgement. Nevertheless, this is
    Something to be thought of, a reality of a kind.

MOSES. Like adultery.

MIRIAM.   Offer of a generalship?
    Of course I don't understand. But like adultery?
    To be a general? Do you mean us to think
    You would refuse—

MOSES.   You both would like to see
    Your brother fat, but your brother has a fancy
    To be as lean as Israel.

MIRIAM.   Where do you see
    Israel now?

MOSES.   Where do I see God?
   Be certain, Israel is. I am here to be a stone
   In her sling, out of her gall.

RAMASES.   Will you promise to be patient?
   There will be difficulties to be got over;
   I have a father. But at some future time
   When I am Pharaoh—

MOSES.   By then I may be free
   To let my bones talk of their disinterest
   In the world's affairs: and whether it is Hebrew
   Or Egyptian, man will cry for me no longer.

MIRIAM. Listen!

AARON.   What is it?

MIRIAM.   Nothing, nothing—I imagined—
   Why should he be back at this time? What
   Could bring him now? Listen!

MOSES.   What do you hear?

MIRIAM. It's the whistle he gives when he's reaching home.

AARON.   Her son.
   It's Shendi.

MIRIAM.   Something has happened. The negro lynx
   Was in my sleep last night praying to become
   A man, but only dead birds came out of its mouth.
   Why is the palace here? What are you doing here
   In my home? He cannot even come home.

RAMASES.   Is this
   Egypt?

MIRIAM. Do you hear him again? No nearer, no nearer.
He is being prevented. Can I get to him
Without being seen? Stay where you are. No one
Must see me, no one.

[*She goes out. In a moment* AARON *follows her*

RAMASES.   You all think of me
As an enemy.

MOSES.   We're not enemies so much
As creatures of division. You and I,
Ramases, like money in a purse,
Ring together only to be spent
For different reasons.
There will be summers to come
Which need the lotus.

RAMASES. Am I never to see you?

MOSES.   No,
It would be better, never. Forget me, Ramases.

RAMASES. That anyway is impossible. I know
I bear your mark, and how will you obliterate
That? Do you forget the feel of the year
When you were as I am? They count me as a man,
Just. But the boy is still in my head and mouth.
I feel him there. I speak him. I should burn
Throne and lotus gladly if I could break
Myself of boyhood, if burning would do it. But you
Are clear and risen roundly over the hazes.
You have the formula. I need it.

MOSES.   Clear?
Evidence of that! Where in this drouthy
Overwatered world can you find me clarity?
What spirit made the hawk? a bird obedient

[27]

To grace, a bright lash on the cheek of the wind
And drawn and ringed with feathered earth and sun,
An achievement of eternity's birdsmith. But did he
Also bleak the glittering charcoal of the eyes
And sharpen beak and claws on his hone of lust?
What language is life? Not one I know.
A quarrel in God's nature. But you, at least,
Are pronounceable: heir of Egypt, heir of Egypt.
That is yourself.

RAMASES.   You mean I'm of no value
Except to be Egypt's ornament.

MOSES.   Of much
Value; infinite.

RAMASES.   But we stay unfriendly?

MOSES. Because I taste your boyhood and remember mine
And like them both.

RAMASES.   But even so—

MOSES.   You shall stay as you are.

RAMASES. Exactly as I am, a friend of Moses.

MOSES. They're coming with Shendi. Keep with me in the shadow.

Enter MIRIAM *and* AARON, *supporting* SHENDI

MIRIAM. He has been so strong. Are you ill? How are you ill?
You can speak, surely you can speak? We don't know them;
That's what is worst—our own—even in childhood
They say so little.

AARON.   Lie here, Shendi.

MIRIAM.   Still
And quiet. What shall I do for him?

AARON.   Give him this water.

MIRIAM. A sip, and then you shall have more.

[28]

SHENDI. They'll come.

MIRIAM. Keep yourself quiet.

SHENDI. Yes, they will come,
They'll come for me, they'll find me!

AARON. What have you done?

MIRIAM. Done?

SHENDI. What are you holding me for? Must I always
Be held? It was the sun! Don't you know that?
They make madmen in the sun. Thousands of madmen
Have been made in the sun. They say nothing, nothing at all,
But suddenly they're running—no, not they,
It's only their bodies that are running: the madmen
Are still standing in the sun, watching their bodies
Run away. Can they kill me for that? Or what, or what?
It was the strike that made it happen!

AARON. What have you said?
What strike?

MIRIAM. He's ill!

SHENDI. No, it was the sun; not the strike,
The sun. The noise of the strike, the whips.

AARON. The strike?
What was it? What has happened?

SHENDI. The spermy bastards!
They make us hit the earth like spit.

MIRIAM. What are you saying?
Don't ask him any more!

AARON. I'll make him tell me. What strike?
What has happened?

[29]

SHENDI. I don't know what has happened.
The brickmakers began it. A youngster was with me,
Twelve years old, and he left me to watch the trouble.
I saw them take him away, they dragged him off
To the captain at the gate, because he was watching.
It has nothing to do with it. It's the sun. Have you heard
The order? They'll not give us straw to make the bricks;
We must gather the straw ourselves; but the tale of bricks
Must be more, more! What does it matter? Who says
It matters? They're coming for me.

MIRIAM. It cannot happen,
Shendi, it cannot.

MOSES. Cannot happen, cannot be.
Cannot. Earth, life, ourselves are impossibility;
What is this Pharaoh who answers me with this?

SHENDI. Who's that?
My uncle, is it? The great fellow that was.
The man who thought he was Egypt. Have you come
To try again, murderer? Look at your crop of relations
And how they do in the land you dunged for us.
Never mind. You did very well.—Oh, what will happen?
Do you hear that? They're whipping the side of the tent.
You know I can't stand up, they've come for me,
You know it was the sun—uncle, uncle!

MIRIAM. It was neighbours talking, it was only the neighbours.
—Aaron,
It was neighbours talking. Wasn't it, wasn't it?

Enter TWO OVERSEERS
No, no!

1ST OVERSEER. Nice family. Here's the man we want.

[30]

2ND OVERSEER.   Get up,
    Little rat. So you'd strike? We'll teach you striking.
    Striking's our specialty. Eh? Not bad! We'll strike him!

MIRIAM. He's sick—can't you see?

1ST OVERSEER.   That's enough of that.

RAMASES.   What is this?
    Weren't you told I had sent for him?

2ND OVERSEER.   My crimes!

RAMASES. Well, weren't you told?

1ST OVERSEER.   No, sir; no, your holiness; not told.
    I beg pardon, sir. I didn't see you, my lord, didn't see you.

RAMASES. I tell you now. I sent for him. Go away.

1ST OVERSEER. Yes, lord.

2ND OVERSEER.   Yes, almighty.

                        [They back away out of sight

MIRIAM. You're here, Shendi, you're here. The prince has kept
    you.
    He spoke for you. Forgive me, I'm more afraid than ever.
    Forgive me. Relief is very like an illness.

SHENDI. No one warned—What are you doing with me?
    Is it a trick? What did I say before they came?
    My lord, I was ill. I don't know what is happening.

RAMASES. Nothing is happening. You can rest.

AARON.   For us
    Much is happening. I begin to have hope.
    Eh, Moses? This is the boy who will be our man,
    The palace key. In the belly of our misfortune
    We find our hope.

[31]

MOSES.   We're not ready to hope
   Or to despair; not ready to doubt or to believe.
   We're equipped to do no more than confront ourselves.
   And if we were equipped for more, hoping
   Or despairing, I wouldn't use him. My need is something
   Different: I need to know how good
   Can be strong enough to break out of the possessing
   Arms of evil. Where shall I look for triumph?
   Somewhere, not beyond our scope, is a power
   Participating but unharnessed, waiting
   To be led towards us. Good has a singular strength
   Not known to evil; and I, an ambitious heart
   Needing interpretation. But not through this boy,
   Never through this boy. I will not use him!

CURTAIN

SCENE THREE

A room in the Palace, giving on to the terrace of Scene One. ANATH *is
standing on the terrace.* TEUSRET'S *voice is heard calling 'Ramases!
Ramases!' It draws nearer.* ANATH *comes into the room and listens
for* TEUSRET'S *voice which now comes from farther away. She turns
to go back to the terrace. Enter* RAMASES.

ANATH. Have you seen him?

RAMASES.   Moses?

ANATH.   Have you seen your father?

RAMASES. He made me a present of my future, with the royal seal
   Attached. Did you know?

ANATH.   I wish you happiness.
   Teusret is looking for you.

[32]

RAMASES.   Where is she?

ANATH.   Everywhere.
  Put your hand in one place, she is already
  Beating her wings in another.

RAMASES.   Listen—look—
  What is this 'now', the moment we're now crossing?
  Can this truth vanish?
  Look, your shadow thrown over the chair,
  That dog's jerking bark, the distance of whistling,
  A gate clanging-to, the water thrown into the yard,
  Your fingers travelling your bracelet, my voice—listen,
  My voice—your breathing—

                [TEUSRET *is heard calling* RAMASES

            And Teusret running through the empty rooms.
  It is true for us now, but not till now, and never
  To be again. I want it for myself.
  This is my life.

                Enter TEUSRET

        It has gone.

TEUSRET.   I've found you at last.
  Where have you been hidden? Where were you?

RAMASES.   With father.

TEUSRET. For an hour!
  No one could tell me. The rooms were all deserted.
  Just as it happens in my sleep sometimes; but then
  The door on the other side of the room is always
  Closing behind you, and the room is empty—I never
  Come to you.

RAMASES.   But, awake, it's different. You find me.

TEUSRET. Why did he talk for so long?

D   [33]

RAMASES.   I'm to be married
   He says.

TEUSRET. I had a riddle to ask you. Fareti
   Taught it to me.

RAMASES.   What is it?

TEUSRET.   Ramases,
   When will you be married?

RAMASES.   Soon, he says.

TEUSRET. Why? Why? You can't! What does he mean?
   Then—if you did—Why have you said so? Oh,
   Why did you say it?

RAMASES.   Teusret—

TEUSRET.   Who is it?

RAMASES.   The Syrian.
   Her name is Phipa.

TEUSRET.   Do you think that's pretty?
   Phipa, Phipa, Phipa! The noise a flute makes
   When the mouth's too full of saliva. You won't do it.

RAMASES. What can I say?

ANATH.   Teusret, we all, you will find,
   Belong to Egypt: our lives go on the loom
   And our land weaves. And the gods know we need
   Some such alliance. If the dynasty is safe
   We can at least be partly ourselves. He will need
   Both of us still.

TEUSRET.   He won't. He will be changed.
   The days will be different and I shall be the same.
   How shall I be happy then?

                        Enter SETI

                            Will *you* be?

   Are you glad?

                          [34]

SETI.   Can you imagine, Teusret,
    The frantic compulsion which first fetched man forming
    And breathing out of the earth's dust? Such
    A compulsion of beauty has this Phipa of Syria,
    With the addition of wit and a good head for business.
    She's immensely rich. Homegoing sailors,
    When there are no stars, steer perfectly for Syria
    Merely by thinking of her. So they say.
    A figure of her, hung under the stern
    And kissing the wake, ensures a harvest of fish.

TEUSRET. What a tale!

SETI.   Well, yes, but she has beauty.

TEUSRET.   Flowers for Ramases
    Then! We must make it an occasion. I'll fetch my lute
    And celebrate. Garlands! I'll make you into
    A nice little afternoon god. Don't go away.

RAMASES. Here, Teusret—

TEUSRET.   You have earned a ceremony.
    Would you rather have me in tears? This isn't silliness
    But a proper formality. I need to do it.
    Wait, all of you.   [*Exit* TEUSRET

ANATH.   Let her do what she must.

RAMASES.   Father,
    I have something to ask you. It has to do with Moses.

SETI. He needn't trouble you.

RAMASES.   Nor any of us. But haven't you
    Overlooked his nephew?

SETI.   This is nothing to you.
    Nothing to you at all.

[35]

RAMASES.   Nothing at all.
  Moses has a sister and a nephew.
  The nephew's a labourer. Might there not here be a way
  By which you could come at Moses?

SETI.   Statesmanship,
  My son, is the gods' gift to restrain their own
  Infidelities to man. As for Moses,
  I'll comprehend him when he's comprehensible.

RAMASES. Such as a commission for this nephew; or a place in the
    palace.
  What do you say? Can you talk of honours
  To a man whose family is unhonoured? I don't know,
  But you will know.

SETI.   Who told you to speak of him?
  What do you know of this name that you're bandying? Anath?
  Is this your influence?

ANATH.   Am I a planet,
  To be so influential? No, Seti; it is not.
  I would rather infect him with something less dubious
  Than the blood of Moses.

                    Enter TEUSRET *with a lute and flowers*

TEUSRET.   Look, I have them. I got them
  Out of my room. They were round my bronze Isis.
  Shall I have offended her?

SETI.   Do you know this nephew?

ANATH. I've seen him.

SETI.   How did he promise?

ANATH.   He promised to be male,
  As though he might have the ability for a beard
  I thought.

                         [36]

TEUSRET. Are you all ready for the ceremony?
Ramases, you must be in a chair; this chair.

RAMASES. Can it be tried?

SETI.   What is it now?

RAMASES.   To mark
My coming of age. May I commission the nephew?

SETI. That is still to be known. I must have precise
Information of him. Now forget the question.
The window on the east side of your room
Is the window that looks toward Syria.

TEUSRET.   Why must you go
Before you see Ramases in flowers? And when
Have you ever heard me play on my lute?   [*Exit* SETI
                           Has no one
Told him he has a daughter?

ANATH.   The flowers were schooled
With salamanders, to be so enduring
In this furnace.

RAMASES.   Will he really do it?

ANATH.   The land
Is rocking, remember. He'll take hold even of grass.

TEUSRET. Let me begin. Neither of you has any sense
Of occasion. These on your shoulders. What *are* flowers?
What is the bridge to be crossed, I wonder,
From a petal to being a wing or a hand? These
For your brows. Does the scent of them sicken you?
My pollen fingers.

RAMASES.   They're shattering already.

TEUSRET. Some of them are too full.

[37]

RAMASES. You've brought me the garden.
　　Here's an earwig on my hand.

TEUSRET. Tread on it. Now
　　You're ripe to receive a god. Isn't he, Aunt?
　　Does he look noble? My brother in bloom.

RAMASES [*treading on the earwig*]. Out goes he. Let's get your sing-
　　ing over.

TEUSRET [*staring*]. I have to remember you. Sing with me.

ANATH. I?
　　Sing? With the crack in my voice? Not songs for bridegrooms.
　　Only songs in the minor, where a false note
　　Can be taken to be excessive sensibility.

TEUSRET. Nothing, nothing will go on in the old way.
　　I wonder, can I remember which is the key? [*She touches the lute*

RAMASES. Did you know my father had ordered the Israelites
　　To gather their own straw?

ANATH. Yes, I knew.

RAMASES. Why did he?

ANATH. A little show of invulnerability.

RAMASES. Is Moses safe here?

TEUSRET. I wish there were echoes in this room,
　　A choir of them, to be company for my voice.
　　You will have to help me when I lose myself.
　　[*Sings*] 　　Why should there be two
　　　　　　Where one will do,
　　　　Step over this shadow and tell me
　　　　　And my heart will make a ring
　　　　　　Sighing in a circle
　　　　And my hands will beckon and bring
　　　　　The maiden fortune who befell me
　　　　　　O fortune, fortune.

[38]

You see, father,—doesn't he look married already?

[*Sings*]   Why do we breathe and wait
          So separate?
      The whirl in the shell and the sand
        Is time going home to time
             Kissing to a darkness.
    So shall we go, so shall we seem
        In the gardens, hand in hand.
          O fortune, fortune.
    So changed against the sun—

    [*She is interrupted by* MOSES, *who enters bearing in his arms
    a dead Israelite boy*

ANATH. What are we to have now?

RAMASES.   The wrong of a right.

SETI. What is this? Isn't it enough that you broke
Into Egypt unasked but you must—

MOSES.   This is your property.
Of little value. Shall I bury it in your garden?
You need have no anxiety. It will not grow.

ANATH. Oh, in the name of the gods—

SETI.   Is your reason gone?

MOSES [*laying the body at* SETI's *feet*]. Look: worthless, worthless.
The music needn't stop.
You killed him.

SETI.   As I thought; you've let your brain
Suffer in this heat. I saw, in the first few words
You spoke this morning, it would end in this.

TEUSRET. Ramases!

SETI. You frighten children, you see.
It's too ambitious.

TEUSRET. That boy!

RAMASES. That isn't death
Lying on the ground.

TEUSRET. It is! It is! It is!

SETI. Well? Tell me: is it an act of sanity
To carry this child here? I'm sorry to see it.
Take him and have him buried. You know it wasn't
Done by me.

MOSES. It was done of you. You'll not
Escape from yourself through the narrows between By and Of.
Your captain killed him on the metal of your gates, as with
A score of others. If it wasn't done of you
Fetch the captain, condemn him to death, and watch
How he'll stare.

SETI. I'll see the man. It's understood.

MOSES. Who understands? And what is understood?
If you move your foot only a little forward
Your toe will be against your power. Is this
How you imagined your strength to be—ungrowing,
Unbreathing, a child, and dead? Out of him
Comes your army, your fleet, the cliff of gold
You move on, pride, place, adulation
And name—out of this contemptible chrysalis—
Not this, not even this, but this destroyed,
This refused to itself. Fetch in your captain,
Fetch in your thousand captains, and condemn them
For the murder of your power.

[40]

SETI.   Nature is lavish,
    And in return for being understood,
    Not hoarded, gives us civilization.
    Would you have the earth never see purple
    Because the murex dies? Blame, dear Moses,
    The gods for their creative plan which is
    Not to count the cost but enormously
    To bring about.

MOSES.   And so they bring about
    The enormity of Egypt. Is that the full
    Ambition of your gods? Egypt is only
    One golden eruption of time, one flying spark
    Attempting the ultimate fire. But who can say
    What secrets my race has, what unworked seams
    Of consciousness in mind and soul? Deny
    Life to itself and life will harness and ride you
    To its purpose. My people shall become themselves,
    By reason of their own god who speaks within them.
    What I ask is that I may lead them peaceably
    Into the wilderness for a space, to find
    Their god and so become living men at last.

SETI. More favours, something new. What god is this?

MOSES. The inimitable patience who doesn't yet
    Strike you down.

SETI.   He and I have something in common
    If he has patience. My trust is Egypt
    And the maturity of the world.

MOSES. You know well enough invasion is probable,
    Unrest is in and out of doors, your southern half
    Splits from the north, the lords at your table
    Are looking down at their hands. And flowing through all

[41]

Is the misery of my blood. Let that be clean
First, and then your flesh may heal.

SETI.   Enough,
I have nursed you enough. Now dungeons can nurse you.
Your god can find you behind the walls
And return your reason when he will.

ANATH. Seti! Are you sure? Will the surly half
Of Egypt believe he was mad?

SETI.   Do you still play
At being his mother?

ANATH.   Do you think I do?

RAMASES. There could have been some other way than this.
Is only Israel present to you,
As once it was only Egypt?
Are you still Moses? Or who? Who are you?

ANATH. Does he know?

SETI.   A man without laws.

MOSES.   What are the laws,
Other than those laws, stupendous and balancing,
Which made the hurl of smiting, infamous fires
Wheel in perfection, perpetually,
In great unaltering constellations:
What are the laws? Tell me, you taker of lives!
I am here by fury and the heart. Is that not
A law? I am here to appease the unconsummated
Resourceless dead, to join life to the living.
Is that not underwritten by nature? Is that
Not a law? Do not ask me why I do it!
I live. I do this thing. I was born this action.
Who can say for whom, for what ultimate region
Of life? A deed is what it becomes.

Despite you, through you, upon you,
I am compelled.

> [*A distant long cracking sound of thunder.* MOSES *jerks back his head to listen*

                         Are we overheard? Behind
The door that shuts us into life, there is
An ear.

ANATH.   The mountains are breaking the drought at last!

MOSES. It is not as we suppose!
What league have we, the human, with the greater
Than human? Am I given the power
To do what I am?
What says the infinite eavesdropper?

> [*From horizon to horizon the sky is beaten into thunder*

CURTAIN TO ACT ONE

ACT TWO

SCENE ONE

MIRIAM'S *tent, the evening of the same day.* MOSES. AARON.

MOSES.   Look: I shall divide them
Into groups a hundred or a hundred and fifty strong,
Each with a man to lead them, one they can trust,
Such as this man you mention, Morshad—
And the man I spoke with this evening. Put them down.

AARON. Morshad and Zedeth. Yes, I have them.

MOSES.   And then
This morning's rioting, the man who started that,
Whatever his name is. Will they listen to him again?

                    [AARON *goes to the tent-opening and looks out*

He made his move too early, some few days
Too soon.

AARON.   I thought I felt the earth quiver.

MOSES. What is he called?

AARON.   The earth has moved. It stirred
Like an animal. Moses!

MOSES.   The man has a name. Put him down.

AARON. Something unnatural has come awake
Which should have slept until time was finished.
Listen! Did you hear a roar? A building
Has collapsed. The dust is like a cloud, higher
Than the city. Will you see?

[44]

MOSES.   We have something more to do
  Than to listen to falling cities. The dust will settle
  While we Hebrews die. Come on; give me the names.

AARON. Why does this mean nothing to you?
  Why won't you come and see it?

MOSES.   The names, the names.

                [MIRIAM *stands in the opening, with a pitcher*

MIRIAM. All the water is blood.

AARON.   Miriam! What is happening to the city?

MIRIAM. There's no water, no water. Nothing but blood.

AARON. Then my fear has foundation. The sun has set
  On truth altogether. The evening's a perjury!
  Let none of us be duped by it.

MIRIAM.   Did you really
  Believe the world? So did we all. The water
  Is blood. The river floods it over the fields.
  The wells stink of it.

AARON.   What are you saying?

MIRIAM.   Go out then
  And see it yourself. The men who were thirsty enough
  To drink what came, are lying at the well-heads
  Vomiting.

MOSES.   What men? Ours?

MIRIAM.   Egyptians.

MOSES.   Miriam,
  What have you there?

MIRIAM.   I filled my pitcher. We all
  Filled our pitchers, everyone, in spite of—

Do you think it could happen to us? To them
Perhaps, something might happen; to the others but not
To ourselves.

MOSES [*bringing his hand out of the pitcher*]. Not to ourselves. To
the others.

MIRIAM.   Your hand
Has water on it! It is water!

MOSES.   From which well
Was this drawn?

MIRIAM.   Our own. Are we likely to use the Egyptians'?
But I saw it, we all saw it.

MOSES.   The sun this last hour
Has been that colour. Doesn't it at evening
Fall directly on our well?

MIRIAM.   The sun? Are we
Talking about the sun? Tell me I'm lying
And look at my feet. We slopped in blood flooding
From the Nile. I saw the Egyptians who drank it.

MOSES.   The Nile.
The Egyptians! But this water came from our well
Not theirs.—Was I waiting, Aaron? I was waiting
Without expectation. But surely, I already knew?
We with our five bare fingers
Have caused the strings of God to sound.
Creation's mutehead is dissolving, Aaron.
Our lives are being lived into our lives.
We are known!

MIRIAM.   Do you think it was you who made the Egyptians
Vomit? We may as well all be mad.
Where is Shendi?

[46]

AARON.   What's this?
Isn't there confusion enough? Confusion I call it!
A contradiction of what we have always known
To be conclusive: an ugly and impossible
Mistake in nature. And you, you of all men
Accept it, identify yourself with it. It must be
Denied. What has become of you since yesterday?
Is it not possible still to be plain men
Dealing with a plain situation? Must we see
Visions? You were an unchallengeable leader once.
That is the man I follow. A plain soldier.

MIRIAM. Where can Shendi be?

MOSES. The plainest soldier is sworn to the service of riddles.
Our strategy is written on strange eternal paper.
We may decide to advance this way or that way
But we are lifted forward by a wind
And when it drops we see no more of the world.
Shall we live in mystery and yet
Conduct ourselves as though everything were known?
If, in battle upon the sea, we fought
As though on land, we should be more embroiled
With water than the enemy. Are we on sea
Or land, would you say?

AARON.   Sea? Land? For pity's sake
Stay with reality.

MOSES.   If I can penetrate
So far.

MIRIAM. What will you do for us? Not as much
As sleep will do, if there is any way
We can come at sleep. Do you think that we
Can sink fear in that water in the pitcher?

[47]

Why hasn't Shendi come home yet? It's past his time.
He should have stayed here the rest of the day.
Will you let me out of this intolerable night?
Are we going to stand here for ever?

SHENDI [*in the tent-opening*].   Mother!

MIRIAM.   Shendi,
Has nothing happened to you? Let me see you and be
Reassured. Were you harmed by what I saw?

SHENDI. What have you seen? Nothing happened? Everything!
We've stepped across to a new life. Where were we living?
It was the appearance, of course, the appearance of hell.
Nothing like it at all, except in our minds, our poor
Minds. I was going to make you try to guess,
But such an idea could never come at a guess.
Never; it couldn't. They've made me an officer!

MIRIAM. I don't—understand what you mean.

SHENDI.   Your son! You see?
They've made him an officer. Like an Egyptian officer.
Like? I am one. We didn't know, that was all,
The world is perfectly fair, something to laugh at.
The ridiculous difference between me this morning
And now! They found I was better with head than hands.

MIRIAM. Shendi, did you come by way of the wells? Did you see
them?

SHENDI. I expect so. They say they're diseased. Can you imagine
How I felt when they took me by the arm and led me
Apart from the other men? I almost fought them.
I knew I was going to be beaten—

MIRIAM.   Shendi, stop!
What are you saying?

[48]

SHENDI.   Hell is done, done,
  Done with, over!

MOSES.   For you.

MIRIAM.   They would never do it.
  But then tonight everything is to be believed.
  Nothing has any truth and anything is true.

SHENDI. I report at the officer's quarters
  In half an hour. I'll take some of my things
  Along with me now. Has the world always been known
  To spring such wonders, do you think? You're to live with me,
  Mother, do you understand? Follow on later
  And ask for the new officer. At the officers' quarters.
  Have you something you can give me to wrap this linen in?
  The Libyans have broken across the border and massacred
  Two companies of the border regiment.

AARON.   What?
  A massacre? When was this?

SHENDI.   I don't know when.
  Where have you put my razor? Four hundred Egyptians
  Killed, they say. They talked as though
  I were already one of themselves. They say
  There's also a rumour of revolution in the south.

AARON. Moses, do you hear?

SHENDI.   Where is my razor?

MIRIAM.   There.
  Did you see the wells? I don't know what life's doing.
  I don't know how we're to think.

AARON.   Ambitiously.
  These incidents all march our way. The Libyans
  Over the border—revolution—Time

E

Is preparing for us with a timely unrest.
We came to Egypt at the perfect hour as it happens.

SHENDI. That's enough of talk like that!

MIRIAM.   As it happens;
If we knew what happens. Shendi an officer!
Will this be what we want, at last? As the Nile
Happens into blood. Shendi an officer.

SHENDI. And the officers' quarters, remember: comfort.

MIRIAM.   As massacre
And revolution happens. As tomorrow
Happens, whatever happens tomorrow.

SHENDI.   Come on,
I must go.

MOSES.   Refuse this commission.

SHENDI.   What did you say?

MOSES. Refuse this commission.

MIRIAM.   Refuse it?

SHENDI.   Listen to that!
As my uncle happens, this is no surprise.
Only one of the family must rise
And glow in Egypt. The rest of us can keep
Against the ground, and lose the whole damned world
Because Moses prefers it. But in spite of that,
In spite of that, generous brother of my mother,
We hope to live a little.

AARON.   As who does not?
The Pharaoh, I quite see, will have his motives.
But we can outmove motives to our advantage;
And here surely is a kind of proffered hand.

[50]

MIRIAM. Why should he refuse? How could he refuse? He
    couldn't.
    But who except you would say he should?

SHENDI.   It's clear
    Why he says it. It was he who came back for recognition
    And I have got it.

MOSES.   Make yourself live, then, Shendi;
    But be sure it is life. The golden bear Success
    Hugs a man close to its heart; and breaks his bones.
    What have they said, these Egyptians?
    Come with us and we'll treat you well.
    Not, come with us and we will treat
    You and your people well.

AARON.   They will come in time
    Even to say that.

SHENDI [to MOSES]. This sounds well
    Indeed, from you!

MIRIAM.   Shendi is to be all
    That he can become—all; and I say so,
    I who made him. Am I to go on holding
    The guilt for his unhappiness when opportunity
    Offers to deliver me from it? Guilt it was,
    And damnation, for giving him birth. This will let me loose!

SHENDI. Why do we listen to him? I know how to value
    The first fairness I've known. If you think so little
    Of being alive, uncle, you will find they're assembling
    Spears to flash on Libya. Why not make something
    Of that? The tradition is that, once upon a time,
    You didn't know the meaning of apprehension
    Or fear—back in those days when it was you
    They treated well.

ANATH [*in the tent-opening*]. Does he still not apprehend
  Or fear?

SHENDI. Madam, madam—

ANATH.   What are you doing
  To Egypt, Moses?

MOSES.   What have you come for?

ANATH.   You.
  What are you doing to Egypt, Moses?

MOSES.   What
  Is Egypt doing to Egypt?

ANATH.   Or Egypt to you.
  Come with me. I came by the old walks.
  What have I seen? You shall come with me
  And see it and tell me, and see the men and women
  Bewildered in the doorways, for the name of their world
  Has changed from home to horror. And is this
  What you have in your heart for Egypt? Then favour me
  And also have it in your eyes.

MOSES.   But why
  Do you come to me? To whose blood has the Nile
  Turned? It isn't mine. Can it be the spilt blood
  Of Israelites that is flowing back on Egypt?
  Why come to me?

ANATH.   He wants reason! Rationalize
  The full moon and the howling dog. I have less
  Inclination to be here than the dog has to howl.
  If you come with me to Seti, he's ready to talk to you.

MOSES. We've talked already.

ANATH.   He'll let you take your Hebrews
  To make their worship, or whatever you want of them,
  On some conditions which he'll tell you.

[52]

AARON.   Good.
   Events are moving.

MOSES.   If Seti is so ready,
   Why did you make the walk through the ominous evening
   To remind me that I'm in Egypt?

ANATH.   Because he is sitting
   Pressing his thumbs together, wedged inactive
   In between his decision and pride. What it is
   To have to do with men! They live too large.
   I'm ready to take you.

MOSES. I'll go.

AARON.   This will be a great day for Israel.

MIRIAM. My son has been made an officer.

ANATH.   I shall be glad
   Not to be alone this time, with the earth
   Wavering to a hint of doom. I suppose
   There have to be powers of darkness, but they should keep
   To the rules. The sky is lighter. The worst may be over.

MOSES. Aaron, you will come too.

AARON.   It has been easier
   Than I should have thought possible this morning.

                    [*Exeunt* ANATH, MOSES, *and* AARON

SHENDI. What is this business the Pharaoh has with my uncle?

MIRIAM. I mustn't think of Moses. Many things
   I must be sure to keep my thoughts quite away from.
   What is it we have to do? A dark mind
   And he has followed that woman.

SHENDI. Will he try to stop my commission going through?

MIRIAM. No, no, he's forgotten it.

                    [53]

SHENDI.   What does he matter, then?
  I'm an officer!

MIRIAM.   How could the water be blood, Shendi?

SHENDI. What?

MIRIAM.   I'll put your things together for you.
  How grand we shall be!

CURTAIN

SCENE TWO

A room in the Palace. SETI.   ANATH.

ANATH. Keep the window covered, Seti. The terrace
  Crackles with dying locusts. I looked out.
  I seemed to look within, on to myself,
  When I stood there and looked out over Egypt.
  The face of all this land is turned to the wall.
  I looked out, and when I looked to the north I saw
  Instead of quiet cattle, glutted jackals,
  Not trees and pasture but vulture-bearing boughs
  And fields which had been sown with hail. And looking
  To the south I saw, like falling ashes after fire,
  Death after thirst, death after hunger, death
  After disease. And when I looked to the east
  I saw an old woman ridding herself of lice;
  And to the west, a man who had no meaning
  Pushing thigh-deep through drifts of locusts.

SETI. Well; these things are finished.

ANATH.   And what happens
  Now? What will you do when the mourners have done

[54]

Wailing, and men look across the havoc of their fields
And the bones of their cattle and say: You did this,
What happens now?

SETI.   Why am I to be blamed
  For all the elemental poisons that come up fungoid
  Out of the damps and shadows which our existence
  Moves in? Can I put peace into the furious
  God-epilepsy of earthquake and eruption?
  What am I but one of those you pity?

ANATH. You tricked him, you tricked Moses, and not once
  But seven times. First when I, against
  All my self-warning, approached the unapproachable
  And brought him to you. Didn't you make him promises
  Then, and break them? And that night your promises
  Plagued our ears with a croaking mockery,
  With an unceasing frog-echo of those words
  Which had meant nothing; with a plague of frogs!
  A second time you made promises, and a third time
  And a fourth: seven times you've broken them
  While the stews of creation had their way with Egypt.

SETI. You say this, concoct this legend; you have become
  Infected with the venom that's against me.

ANATH. No, I've no venom. I've no more efficacy
  Than a fishwife who has been made to breed against
  Her will; and so I'm shrill and desperate.
  No power against misery! That's what our lives add up to.
  Our spacious affability, our subtle intelligence,
  Our delicate consciousness of worlds beyond the world,
  Our persuasive dignity when sacrificing to the gods,
  Our bodies and our brains can all become
  Slutted with lice between afternoon and evening.
  You tricked him a second time, and that is what

[55]

You saw: sweet made foul. And then the third time
And we became the dungheap, the lusted of flies,
The desirable excretion. Our pleasantness was flyblown.

SETI. I've suffered this once with Egypt—

ANATH.   You tricked Moses.
And what has come of it I would bring back to you
Until pity came out of you like blood to the knife,
Remembering how disease swept all the cattle,
How we could not sleep for intolerable lowing
Till daylight rounded up the herds of wolftorn
Death. You tricked him, and that feculent moment
Filthied our blood and made of us a nation
Loathsome with boils. You had stirred up the muck
Which the sweet gods thought fit to make us of
When they first formed man, the primal putrescence
We keep hidden under our thin dress of health.
What a pretty world, this world of filthmade kings!
When, after the sixth time, the hail came down,
I laughed. The hail was hard, metallic, cold
And clean, beating on us with the ferocity
Of brainbright anger. As cut diamonds, clean,
Clean, and fit to be beaten down by. When
It stamped out the gardens and cracked the skulls of birds
It bruised away the memory of vermin
And struck our faces fairly. If then, if only
Then our consciousness had gone clean out,
Or if then you had let these Israelites go with Moses,
We should not now so vainly
Shuffle our fingers in the dust to find
The name we once were known by. But you tricked
For the seventh time, and then the curse of the locusts
Strangled the whole air, the whole earth,

[56]

Devoured the last leaf of the old life
That we had sometime lived. The land is naked
To the bone, and men are naked beyond the bone,
Down to the barest nakedness which until now
Hope kept covered up. Now climb and sit
On the throne of this reality, and be
A king.

SETI.   Anath! These plagues were not my doing
And you know they were not. No man would say I caused them.
Only a woman with her mind hung
With a curtain of superstition would say so.

ANATH.   I admit it.
I am superstitious. I have my terrors.
We are born too inexplicably out
Of one night's pleasure, and have too little security:
No more than a beating heart to keep us probable.
There must be other probabilities.
You tricked Moses after I had gone myself
To bring him to you, and what followed followed.

SETI. It is true I made certain concessions to Moses
And reconsidered them. I was prepared
To let him have his way, if in return
He would use his great abilities to our advantage.
But am I to have no kind of surety
That he'll return, after this godhunt of his?
I said to him Take the men but their wives and children
Must remain. And then I went further: I told him to take
Both men and women, but the children must stay. And at last
I only insisted on their cattle, since our cattle
Were dead. I'll not be panicked by this chain
Of black coincidence, which he with his genius
For generalship has taken advantage of.

[57]

He presumes upon the eternal because he has
No power to strike his bargain. I have not done
These things to Egypt. I'll not hear it be said.

ANATH. Well, they're done. Blame has no value anyway.
There's not one of us whose life doesn't make mischief
Somewhere. Now after all you've had to give way.
We must calculate again, calculate without Moses.
I picked unhappy days in those girlhood rushes.
But at least we can sweep away the locusts.

SETI.   You understand
There will be no postponement of Ramases' marriage.
We can look forward to that, and the change of policy
Which I shall force presently.

ANATH.   What do you mean?
Moses by now has called the assembly of the Hebrews.
By now Egypt has heard the news. Moses
Has taken policy out of your hands.

SETI.   I sent
Word after him.

ANATH.   Seti! What word did you send?
What have you done?

SETI.   I have only been careful
To protect your future. Even before Moses
Had gone three steps from the palace there came the news
Of another defeat. Fate has taken a hammer
To chip and chip at our confidence.
But while I still have Moses to come at my call
I have not lost him. And while he needs my help
He will continue to come. And when he is tired—
We'll make a bargain.

[58]

ANATH.   All this, then, over again.
   You're mad. It isn't we who make the bargains
   In this life, but chance and time. I tell you it's madness!

Enter RAMASES

RAMASES. Father,
   Is it true you've withdrawn your latest promise to Moses?

SETI. Whatever I have done or not done isn't to be said
   In a sentence.

RAMASES.   They say it's true. Wherever I have gone
   Dank rumour has been rising off the pavements, chilling
   Into the heart of the people: 'Pharaoh has refused
   Moses again. What new disastrous day
   Is coming?' I tell you I've been out walking
   Under the burning windows of the people's eyes.
   You've stood fast long enough. Let Moses take
   The Hebrews.

SETI.   So you also are afraid of magic
   And believe that this tall Moses can make a business
   Out of curses? Do you suppose if I surrendered to him
   There would be any less roaring in the wind
   Or less infection in disease? Why
   Aren't you beside me like another man,
   Instead of so fretting me with nursery behaviour
   That I could strike you? I made life in your mother
   To hand me strength when I should need it. That life
   Was you. I made you exactly for this time
   And I find you screeching to escape it.

RAMASES.   I have been
   Through streets that no men should have to walk in.
   You must let the Hebrews go. Father, you must!

SETI. You know nothing, you little fool, nothing! Govern
   By your idiocy when I am dead.

[59]

RAMASES.   What

    Will you leave for me to govern, or what by then
    Shall I have become, what figure of faded purple
    Who clears his throat on an unimportant throne?
    I am to you only the boy who comes
    To the door to say goodnight on his way to bed.
    It's you who invite the future but it's I
    Who have to entertain it, remember that.
    What is expedience for you may become
    Dark experience for me. And these last weeks
    I've heard the future's loping footfall, as plague
    Came after plague, and I knew the steps
    Were not passing but approaching. You
    Were persuading them. They came each time a little
    Nearer, and each time closer to me.
    Keep your word to Moses. Let him take them.

SETI. I tell you it isn't possible.

RAMASES.   Then get

    Yourself another heir, and make him eat
    Your black bread of policy. Marry yourself
    To this girl from Syria. My plans are different.

SETI. Your plans are different! You insolent cub, you spoiled
    Insolent cub! And so your plans are different?
    You've already made your plans!

RAMASES.   Wait. What

    Was that noise?

ANATH.   The old familiar. A man crying out.
    What difference is one man's groaning more or less?

RAMASES [*looking from the terrace*]. Oh horrible! What is it that
    makes men
    And makes them like this man? Abortions of nature.
    It is true what they said.

[60]

ANATH.   What is true?

RAMASES. What the other officers said, what I thought they spread
  About out of malice: that Shendi outstruts them all,
  Drives the Hebrews harder than any Egyptian
  Drives them, hits them down with a readier fist,
  And smiles and thrives under the admiration
  Of the overseers. Go out on the terrace if you doubt me
  And see him, Shendi, the son of Miriam, a Jew
  Beating a Jew.

SETI.   So perhaps at last,
  So perhaps at last you will have seen
  That what you thought was child's play, black and white,
  Is a problem of many sides. And you will kindly
  Wait and learn. This fellow does the work
  Which you yourself suggested he should do
  And does it conscientiously, without sentiment.

RAMASES. I suggested he should do it. Yes.
  I put the whip in his hand. I raised that arm.
  I struck that Jew. I did it. I did not know
  How the things we do, take their own life after
  They are done, how they can twist themselves
  Into foul shapes. I can now see better
  The deathly ground we live on. Yes, all right,
  I have surrendered. Whatever happens will happen
  Without me. I've finished meddling.

ANATH.   Ramases!
  Of all the Jews one Jew has done this.

RAMASES.   It might be
  A thousand instead of one.

ANATH.   Ramases, only
  One Jew!

[61]

SETI. Would you even encourage the traitor
   In my son, because of your fear of this Moses?

ANATH.   Yes,
   I would make him rebellious, and if I could I would make
   Every limb of your body rebellious;
   I'd paralyse that pride which with such cunning
   Packs us into a daily purgatory
   Of apprehension.

SETI.   The purgatory may save you
   From damnation. But turn yourselves all against me.
   I stand now living and breathing only to protect
   This country from disintegration.

ANATH.   Oh
   The gods, how we fumble between right and wrong,
   Between our salvation and our overthrow,
   Like drunk men with a key in the dark who stand
   At the right door but cannot get out of the cold.
   May the moment of accident bless us.

RAMASES.   I shall not
   Rebel again. That will be one trouble less.

SETI. Stand beside me. We're almost of equal height
   And may yet come to be of equal mind;
   And if that is so, one of us will find
   The way of escape out of this distress
   Of ours, either you or I.

                 Enter KEF, *a Minister to the Pharaoh*

KEF.   My lord Pharaoh.
SETI. News; come on.

KEF.   Better to hear it alone.

SETI. Bad news. Well, let's have it. Catastrophe
   Is no longer my secret. Let us have it all.

[62]

KEF. My lord—

SETI.   Go on, go on,

KEF.   A report that the Libyans
Have annihilated the reinforcing fifth
Division.

SETI.   It is impossible.

KEF.   They were surrounded
And surprised. Only six men got through.

SETI.   Six men.

RAMASES. Six men.

SETI.   They make me a pack-horse to carry despair.
They load me to the last inch.

Enter TEUSRET

TEUSRET.   Moses has come
Again. I saw him walking like a lion
Behind bars, up and down in your battered garden,
Ramases. The sentries had tried to hold him
But he broke through their spears as though he didn't see them.
He looked at me, his eyes the colour of anger;
He looked at me and gripped a mulberry-bough
And broke it, and said Go to your father, fetch me
Your father.

SETI.   He can walk longer and break more boughs.
He shall wait, and find that Egypt is hard ground
Under his lion's walk. [*To* KEF] Go out to the overseers
And tell them to tighten discipline, to give
No rest to those Hebrews, not to let man, woman
Or child straighten their backs while they still stand.

[63]

I shall not see him until I choose; and, when
I choose, for his people's sake, he'll do what I need.
See this done.

ANATH.   Seti, take care; take care
What you do.

SETI.   Let Moses think again what behaviour
Is best, best to save his people.   [*Exit*

TEUSRET.   Ramases,
What is it? Why are you so silent? Are you afraid
As well? Are you afraid? Are you, Ramases?

RAMASES. Why should I be? The sweet part of the world's
All over, but that's nothing. It had to go.
My mind had lutes and harps and nodding musicians
Who drowned my days with their casual tunes. They have been
Paid off by this honest hour. And now I hear
My voice raised in deathly quiet. It's insufferable
That my voice, without the accompaniment of good fortune,
Should be so out of key, so faltering,
So cracking with puberty.—Aunt Anath,
What's the meaning of my manhood, to be found
So helpless, to be so helpless: what is there to do
Which I could do and haven't yet seen?

ANATH. We're no longer alone.

                    [MOSES *stands in the doorway*

TEUSRET.   Look, Ramases.

MOSES.   Where is Seti?

ANATH. He will not see you.

MOSES.   When will he learn? When,
When, when will he learn? We have agonized
This land with anger for too many days.

ANATH.   You
   And he together. No birth is worth this labour.

MOSES. For three hundred years the pangs of this coming deliver-
      ance
   Have been suffered by my people, while Egypt played.
   But now Egypt suffers, and she says
   This is a new hell. But hell is old;
   And you yourself sitting in sunlight
   Embroidered on it with your needle. Hell
   Is old, but until now
   It fed on other women, that is all.

ANATH. And all is the innocent as well as the guilty;
   All is the small farmer and the singing fisherman
   And the wife who sweeps; tomorrow's boy as well
   As yesterday's. All these, while Seti twists
   To have his way, must go to your fire like sticks.

RAMASES [*looking from the terrace*]. The gods help them now! The
      gods help those Hebrews!

MOSES. It must be one people or another, your people
   Or mine. You appeal to Moses,
   But Moses is now only a name and an obedience.
   It is the God of the Hebrews, springing out
   Of unknown ambush, a vigour moving
   In a great shadow, who draws the supple bow
   Of his mystery, to loose this punishing arrow
   Feathered with my fate; he who in his hour
   Broke the irreparable dam which kept his thought,
   Released the spumy cataract birth and death
   To storm across time and the world;
   He who in his morning
   Drew open the furious petals of the sun;

F   [65]

He who through his iron fingers
Lets all go, lets all waste and go,
Except, dearly retained in his palm, the soul:
He, the God of my living, the God of the Hebrews,
Has stooped beside Israel
And wept my life like a tear of passion
Onto the iniquity of Egypt.

ANATH. So the great general steps down to captaincy.
I wonder. Does this god use you
Or do you use this god? What is this divinity
Which with no more dexterity than a man
Rips up good things to make a different kind
Of good? For any god's sake, if you came here
To get justice, also give justice.   •
In this mood the lot goes headlong.

MOSES.   Headlong!
And our memories too. And our hands which once
Knew how to come together, must now forever
Hide themselves in our dress. We are utterly separate.

RAMASES. Look at the sky! A sea of cloud, blind-black,
Is pouring on to the beaches of the sun!

TEUSRET. Oh, it will swamp the sailing of the air!
The sky will be gone from us, it's taking the sky!
What shall we do?

ANATH.   Hush, Teusret.

[*The stage grows dark*

MOSES.   Seti
May see better without the light of day.
The hand of God has gone across his eyes
And closed all life upon itself. Egypt

[66]

Goes inward, by a gate which shuts more heavily than sunset,
Leaving man alone with his baffled brain.
Only Seti can let the sun free again.

ANATH. It is here! The darkness!

MOSES.   Tell him, tell Seti
That I wait for his answer.

CURTAIN TO ACT TWO

ACT THREE

SCENE ONE

MIRIAM'S *tent at night*. AARON. *Enter* MIRIAM.

AARON. Everything has been done, I think. I have daubed
The lamb's blood three times over the entry
And all that remained of the meat has been burned.—
Miriam! You; not Moses! What do you want
Here at close on midnight?

MIRIAM. Must I want something
To come into my own tent?

AARON. Tell me; what is it?
There's no time left. Has the news got past our silence?
Do they know? That's why you've come in the night. The Egyptians
Are one ahead of us!

MIRIAM. News? I've got no news.
Is there any news at midnight? I've come to sleep.

AARON. Why not sleep, as you did, in the city with Shendi?

MIRIAM. Do I have to be catechized in my own tent?
If you want to ferret in unlighted places
Penetrate into the mind of Moses, and let me
Sleep.

AARON. His mind will be our history
Before the morning. Whatever is about to happen—
I cannot doubt that something is about to happen—
Will divulge him to us at last. I have become

[68]

Almost docile to his darkness. By what providence
I wonder, did you come back? There was no way
Of getting word to you, but you came, thank God.
Whatever is wrong for you, to make you walk
So far to sleep, this midnight of Moses
(I call it to myself his midnight) will clarify
Into right.

MIRIAM.   Wrong things and right things!
So you still talk of those, those things that are catches
To make us lose heart. Take evil by the tail
And you find you are holding good head-downwards.
Let me go to sleep.

AARON.   Something that Shendi has done
Has brought you back.

MIRIAM.   Shendi, Shendi to blame!
To you Shendi is always blameable.
Because at last he can have ambitions,
Because he's ripping up the bare boards
His boyhood lay on, to make himself a fire
Which will warm his manhood, we turn on him—yes,
I also, as much as you—I stormed so.
I? The right to blame him? The wrong to have borne him
To that childhood. Why shouldn't he be finished with the lot of
    us?

AARON. So he turned you out: he sent you away.

MIRIAM.   I left him.
I came away from him. I couldn't watch him
Live what is now his life.

AARON.   I won't think of him.

MIRIAM. He'll succeed without your thoughts.

AARON.   Look at me, Miriam.

[69]

MIRIAM. You're going away.

AARON.   And so is all Israel.
We all have staves in our hands and our feet shod
For travelling; Moses' orders. He also gave
Other orders; they were very curious.
We have all had to eat lambs' flesh, seasoned
With bitter herbs. As I see it, Miriam,
That is his characteristic way of achieving
Unity among us, before the event,
That we should all fill this waiting time by doing
The same thing, however trivial. And then
We have splashed the blood three times over the doorways.
That is quite inexplicable. It is drying in the night air,
At this moment, while I speak. What happens, I ask myself,
When it is dry? It means our freedom. He has told me so.
Tonight we're to go free. And when I look at him
I have to permit myself a wonderful hope.

MIRIAM. He came back from Midian a madman.

AARON. His madness seems to be a kind of extended sanity.
But he tells me nothing, nothing is discussed or planned
Even with me, his lieutenant. And this closeness
Has hurt me, I won't try to deny it. And yet
He has me by the scruff of the heart and I ask
No questions. I've begun to believe that the reasonable
Is an invention of man, altogether in opposition
To the facts of creation, though I wish it hadn't
Occurred to me. I've been with Moses, watching
How in tent after tent he manipulated
Man upon man into consciousness. Though perhaps
They don't know of what they're conscious, any more than I do.
Except of the night; of the night, Miriam! I would swear
The night is dedicated to our cause.

[70]

You must have seen it: there's such a brightness,
Such a swingeing stillness, the sky has transfixed itself;
As though it hung with every vigorous star
On some action to be done before daybreak.
Is it my nerves? A sort of high apprehensive fever?
I can't discuss myself. Tomorrow this glitter
And piercing peace may be something of our own.

MIRIAM. Peace! Give it to me, for God's sake.
　　All I could see was the peace of the crouching creature
　　Hanging upon its pounce.

Enter SHENDI

SHENDI.　　　　　　　　Why must he be here?
　　I have something to say to you, mother

MIRIAM.　　　　　　　　　Not any more
　　Tonight; nothing more said tonight. Go back
　　To your bed.

SHENDI.　　　Yes, you must listen!

AARON.　　　　　　　　Listen to your tongue
　　Or your brotherly whip?

MIRIAM.　　　　　　He knows already what we feel.
　　Now let him alone.

SHENDI.　　　　　Let him think what he likes. I have come
　　To you, not to him. We've taken so long to get
　　What at last we have: why must you spoil it? I know;
　　It was the spate of our tempers, gone again now.
　　If you go away from me, more than half the triumph
　　Is lost. You haven't been my mother for nothing.
　　I mean to see you happy.

[71]

MIRIAM.   I shall stay alone.

SHENDI. Oh, it's fantastic. What did you expect
My work to be? And how can we be scrupulous
In a life which, from birth onwards, is so determined
To wring us dry of any serenity at all?

MIRIAM. You must do as you must.

AARON.   But in the morning
He may wish he had chosen otherwise.

SHENDI.   What do you mean?
Let me hear what you mean by that. Have you
And your brother done some dirtiness against me
To put me wrong with the Pharaoh? I know you'd founder me
If you had the chance—

Enter MOSES

MOSES.   Get ready. Miriam. And you,
Shendi. Get together all that you value.
You won't come to this tent again.

MIRIAM.   Get ready?
All that I value? What would that be, I wonder?
Tell your delirium to be precise.

AARON. This midnight is his. For pity's sake believe it,
Miriam. Then all our wills resolved into
One Will—

SHENDI.   His, of course! The stupendous mischief
Of the man! I beg your pardon if he no longer
Rates himself as a man after living through
The pestilences as though he owned them.
You can blame him, not me, for the punishment
I give the labourers. He makes them undisciplined
With his raving of freedom which they'll never get.

[72]

It's he, not I, who knits the darker and darker
Frowns for Pharaoh—it's he who's the one for you
To abominate, if anybody.

MOSES.   Be ready for journey.
The time is prepared for us. What we were is sinking
Under the disposition of what will be.
Let it so dispose; let us not fondle our wrongs
Because they're familiar. Now, as the night turns,
A different life, pitched above our experience
Or imagining, is moving about its business.
To-night—Aaron, Miriam, Shendi—our slavery
Will be gone.

AARON.   Do you hear what he says?

MIRIAM.   What is he hiding?
There's something he knows.

AARON.   Something known by the night;
That was how it felt to me.

MIRIAM.   What is it you know?

MOSES.   The sound
Of God. It comes; after all, it comes. It made
The crucial interchange of earth with everlasting;
Found and parted the stone lips of this
Egyptian twilight in the speech of souls,
Moulding the air of all the world, and desiring
Into that shell of shadow, a man's mind—
Into my own.

AARON.   What was told? What was said?

SHENDI.   Oh, leave them
To excite each other. I'm going if you're not.

[73]

MOSES. Stay where you are. Do you deny voice
 To that power, the whirler of suns and moons, when even
 Dust can speak, as it does in Moses now?
 It comes.
 And by the welding of what loved me and what harmed me,
 I have been brought to that stature which has heard.
 Tonight, at midnight,
 God will unfasten the hawk of death from his
 Grave wrist, to let it rake our world,
 Descend and obliterate the firstborn of Egypt,
 All the firstborn, cattle, flocks, and men:
 Mortality lunging in the midnight fields
 And briding in the beds: a sombre visit
 Such as no nation has known before. Upon
 All Egypt! Only we who have the darkness
 Here in our blood, under the symbol of blood
 Over our doors, only we of Israel
 Standing ready for the morning will be unvisited.

AARON. So this is what you know.

SHENDI.   What he wants, what he fondly
 Imagines. Why did I follow you here
 To get drawn into this? That fox has his tail on fire
 And someone should know about it. For the last time,
 Are you coming?

MIRIAM.   Don't go back—not just
 Within a pace of this midnight.

SHENDI.   I can see
 What's been thought out between you. Now that you have me,
 You think you'll keep me: here, dropped back in the pit.
 What a chance of it! Must I tell you that I'm an Egyptian?
 An Egyptian! I'm an Egyptian! Don't I know

[74]

How he's waited for me to slip up, because he
Slipped up?

MOSES.   Break and finish that!
Break that jealous puppet you have dubbed with my name.
That Moses in your head is a lie.

SHENDI. What does it matter whether he is
Or he isn't? You want to bring Egypt down,
To fell her with the weight of her own achievement.
What else but Egypt is able to make birth
A proposition? You aim to destroy excellence
For what you call a justice. Justice
Is the greatness that comes to the great!

MOSES.   It's the crossing of mind
With mind. How can I make you see me, clear
Of what you want to believe?

SHENDI.   I see you well enough.
You've taken ten years looking for the logic of your murder
And now you think you've found it.

AARON.   Midnight, midnight!
Have you forgotten it? No doubt the timing of God
Will be extremely exact. And does nothing, no presentiment,
Creep on the heart of Pharaoh at this moment?

MOSES. Aaron!

AARON. I wonder, does nothing make him fetch his firstborn
Beside him——

MOSES.   Aaron!
Do you see the ambush I have blundered into?
I heard God, as though hearing were understanding.
But he kept his hands hidden from me. He spoke,
But while he spoke he pointed. Aaron, he pointed
At Ramases, and I couldn't see!

AARON.   The boy
    Pays for the father.

MOSES.   Why had I not thought of him?
    I had such tremendous heart. I saw the passion of bewilder-
        ment
    Drawing off from the earth. But can we go forward
    Only by the ravage of what we value? Surely
    I who have been the go-between for God
    Can say that this is not part of my intention
    And be heard?

AARON.   What, at this point? Is this how you fought
    Your other wars? There were boys then who put
    Eager toes into fatal stirrups, who were young
    And out of life altogether in the same
    Almighty and unthinkable moment. You learnt
    Then to grieve and advance, uninterrupted.
    And so it has to be now.

MOSES.   Look what it is.
    God is putting me back with the assassins.
    Is that how he sees me? Does one deed
    Become our immortal shape? And Egypt! Egypt!
    He was meant for Egypt. Aaron,
    You are here in my place until I come again.
    Keep Shendi with you.

AARON.   Where are you going?

MOSES. Keep Shendi with you.   [He goes

AARON. He is in a space somewhere between
    The human and inhuman. That's a terrible
    Neighbourhood.

SHENDI.   Did you see how he looked? He believes ·
    What he said.

[76]

MIRIAM. Shut us in. He has gone.
Can't we forget the man?

SHENDI. I won't stay here!
Thank goodness I can go where things are healthier.

AARON. It's midnight.
Wasn't that the winding of the city's horn,
The sound of twelve? I think so. I have to delay you,
Shendi.

SHENDI [*at the tent-opening*]. Nobody will delay me.

MIRIAM. Stay in the tent!

AARON. The hour may go past and leave us knowing
It was unremarkable. But wait till the light,
Wait, Shendi, keep yourself unseen
By that inquisition of stars out there.
Wait for Moses to return.

SHENDI. Who?

MIRIAM. What is it? What have you seen?

SHENDI. I've lost the city,
I can't reach it! You trapped me!

MIRIAM. What do you see?

SHENDI. The sand is rising and living!
Is an invisible nation going through to the north?
Or what is it the sand can feel? I can't go back,
God, God, I can't go!

MIRIAM. Come inside,
Shendi, come into the tent.

AARON. Happening,
You see, happening. Why try to go back?

[77]

SHENDI. Some of the men will still be awake. We could light
The lights in the barrack-room. If only some of them
Would come out to look for me! Can you hear it, the noise,
The rending apart and shuddering-to of wings?
Where can I get away from this? Nowhere
Except into the ground.

MIRIAM.   Shendi, here, in the tent.
In the tent: it will pass the tent.

AARON [*dragging him in*].   Are you trying to die?

SHENDI. Let me go, death; death, let me go!

AARON.   It is I
Not death.

SHENDI.   It isn't only you.
The wings were right over me and I was wrenched by a hand
That came spinning out of them. I'll not be sent into a grave.
I'll be what I was. I am Shendi, a Jew.
How can my blood alter and make me Egyptian?
I only wanted to be free!   [*He tears off the Egyptian uniform*
Look: Egypt comes away—it's no part of me,
It's easily off. This body is all I am—
It is Shendi, the Jew, Shendi, Shendi, a Jew,
A Jew! Isn't it so? Then why am I dying?

MIRIAM. You are not, Shendi; it's gone past us. There's nothing
more.

AARON. Look, you're with us.

SHENDI.   Only free to die?
This wasn't a world. It was death from the beginning.
Here's my name, without a man to it. My name!
Let me go. It's a chance! I'll make them see me. Wings,
                    [*He breaks away into the dark*

[78]

Shadows, eagles! I am Shendi, Shendi, the Jew!
I am Shendi the Jew! Shendi the Jew!

MIRIAM.   Shendi!
He has gone behind the sand. Son!   [*She runs into the dark*

AARON.   The night
Of deliverance. Tonight we all go free.
And Miriam too. He said she would go free.

> [*The voice of* MIRIAM *is heard crying out her last desperate*
> '*Shendi!*'

CURTAIN

SCENE TWO

The Palace. ANATH. TEUSRET

ANATH. How the stars have taken possession of the sky tonight.

TEUSRET. Occasion, dear Aunt. Phipa is coming,
The magnitude out of Syria.

ANATH.   Tomorrow.

TEUSRET. No; now they say tonight, very soon,
For Ramases. Messengers were here
Half an hour ago, sweating in the cool yard.
She's already at Hahiroth, with her romantic nature
Plying the spurs, and waking all the villages
With the interminable jingle-jangle of what father calls
Her considerable means. We shall see her tonight.

ANATH. How do we welcome her? Nothing has been said
To me.

TEUSRET. Who says anything in this palace now
Except good morning or good night? Father

[79]

Waits for each moment to come and touch him
And then it has gone before he can use it.

ANATH.   And you
Have a hard welcome for this girl from Syria.

TEUSRET. No; I'm praying her here, for all our sakes.
She will bring solid and gay Syria
To chase away the fiends.

Enter SETI
                              Who is that?

SETI. I. Is there something to be seen?

ANATH. We're watching the dark for bridles.

TEUSRET.   And the dark
Watches us. I know you dislike me to be afraid of it.
Are we all to meet her in the jumping shadows,
Aunts, owls, flame, sisters and all?
Or will she go quietly to bed and wait for tomorrow?

SETI. Tonight. She must dismount into a light
Of welcome. Where's your brother? . . . Turn this way;
Are you handsome? Well, the years of my life
Conveyed in a woman, perhaps safely. Remember to love me
For everything you become, particularly
For the worship of the male sunrise which will stand
Over your maturity.

TEUSRET.   What is it, father?
What is it?

SETI.   How many thousand thousand years
Are being nursed in your body, my young daughter?
And under a secure lock, away from the eyes.

TEUSRET. What eyes?

SETI.   The envy; confusion. Do you know
Where to look for Ramases?

[80]

TEUSRET.   He was trying to sleep.
  What is it that's wrong?

SETI.   The world's constitution.
  Otherwise everything is much as we would wish it.
  I'll tell you what is wrong. The world is a wonder
  Married to some deformity; but we'll
  Fetch them apart. Where's Ramases?

TEUSRET.   In bed.

SETI. He can go to bed tomorrow.

ANATH.   Precious heart,
  That was a wild cry that ripped the darkness
  From somewhere down in the city.

SETI. He will have dreams in plenty after tonight;
  I'm giving them to him with both my hands. Where is he?
  Fetch him.

RAMASES [*in the doorway*]. I am here, sir.

SETI.   You're the Pharaoh.

ANATH. Seti!

SETI.   You have slept into a throne and an empire
  While time has begun to heap age over me
  With a bony spade, to make me like the rest,
  Ramases, like the poor rest.

RAMASES.   Has Syria come?

ANATH. Tell the boy what you mean: and me.
  What are you pulling down now?

SETI.   Myself.
  It seems that I have grown too tall
  And keep out the sun. I overbranch the light.
  I am giving you the throne, Ramases.

G   [81]

It gives itself. The wind has hurled it under you,
A biting wind, the hatred that has turned me
Into decay and grub in my own garden.
You may have luckier hands. You have at least
Hands less calloused with enemies. You will be able
To hold the sceptre perhaps without such pain.

ANATH. Abdication!

RAMASES.   Is that what you mean? The throne?

SETI. This is how we distract them: under my seal
   Affixed in the morning, Moses shall have the permission
   He has raged for: and then, with the sun somewhat higher,
   Under my final seal you shall take Egypt.
   I drown myself in my own wave: I am not,
   But I am always. And when they come, the factions,
   The whorers and devourers, roaring over
   The rocks of the dynasty, they'll only find
   Perpetual Egypt.

RAMASES.   I'm to inherit the kingdom
   Of desperate measures, to be not a self
   But a glove disguising your hand. Is there nowhere
   Where I can come upon my own shape
   Between these overbearing ends of Egypt?
   Where am I to look for life?

SETI.   What else
   Am I shaking over you but a wealth of life?
   Do you comprehend, this land, the bright wrists
   Of the world on which the centuries are bracelets,
   Is yours? And the heart of beauty out of Syria.
   Teusret, watch: is there anything to be seen?
   Any sound yet?—Stupidity, what would you have?
   Love is the dominant of life, to which all our changes

Of key are subdued in the end. You will be able
To wander the winding and coitous passages
Of the heart, and be more than you could have prophesied
For yourself.

TEUSRET.   Listen, listen!

SETI.   Is it the girl?

TEUSRET. No, listen!

ANATH.   A tortured gale, a gale
Of crying moving through the streets.

TEUSRET.   Listen!
It's the noise of breaking lives.

SETI.   What is it now?

RAMASES. What is it, Darkness? Why are you coming now?
For whom this time?

ANATH.   Oh, make the city silent!

TEUSRET. Someone's coming: a shadow, a man,
Leaping for the terrace.

RAMASES.   Let it come to me.
If I'm to have Egypt I'll have its treachery, too.
Keep away from the window. Who goes there? Stand.
Who goes there? Who is it?

                    [MOSES *comes breathlessly on to the terrace*

MOSES. Shut all your doors! Nothing will wait for us,
We are at war with this moment. Draw yourselves
Like swords. It is for Ramases.

RAMASES.   For me?

MOSES. Put your lives round him.

SETI.   Have you come
Out of the city? What's there? What's on its way?

MOSES. Death, death, deliberately
 Aimed, falling on all your firstborn sons,
 All Egypt's firstborn, Seti, cattle and men;
 Death particular and infallible, mounting
 With an increasing terrible wake of cries
 To your window, to come to Ramases. I know—
 It was I that loosed it. Can I deflect it now?
 Can we so rope our lives together that we
 Can be a miracle against death?

SETI.   Go back
 Into your night. I'll not believe in you.

ANATH. What do you want from us?

MOSES.   Power of life
 To beat death out of this house.
 The vigour of our lives must be
 The miracle to save him.

ANATH.   What is my life?
 It went to be your shadow. For fifteen years
 It has been nothing but a level of darkness
 Cast on the world by you. I made myself
 Your mother, and then loved you and desired you
 Till you became the best and worst of the world,
 The water that kept me alive to thirst. I
 Was afraid for you to know you were not my son,
 For then I should have lost even that right in you.

MOSES. Anath——

ANATH.   I loved you until I longed to hear
 That you were dead.

MOSES.   Not this, not now!
 Give me greater life for the boy's sake.

ANATH. At last, at last you need something of me. Can
My love for you shield him from death?

RAMASES.   And yet—
And yet, if I'm to live, shall I know how?

SETI. There's life in questions. But pray that you get no answers.
Our power and progress is being free from truth.
Sufficient illusion is sufficient life.
And I've changed the channel that evil was running in:
This boy's the Pharaoh now.

RAMASES.   Is it too late,
No use after all?

MOSES.   More life! The dark
Is already beside us. In life's name, what are we?
Five worlds of separation? Or can we be
Five fingers to close into a hand
To strike this death clean away from us?

RAMASES. Its hand is already passing through my hair
Feeling for the skull.

MOSES.   Has none of us the life
To keep him living?

SETI.   I will do anything
But all direction is gone.

MOSES.   Pain of man,
Affirm my strength, and make me
Equal to this wrestler come against me.

TEUSRET. Look, look—the torches in the gateway;
She is here!

SETI.   Anath, all of you,
We meet her as though Egypt were in high health;
No anxiety on your faces as of ambassadors
Of a haunted country.

[85]

TEUSRET.   We shall be alive again.
Phipa has come to us, and the horns have begun
To wind their welcome in the towers. Come on,
Ramases, come to meet her. The dark's not dangerous
Now.

RAMASES. But still dark. And we have to enact
A daylight for this unsuspecting beauty.
Well, we'll meet her.

ANATH.   No, don't go, don't look!
The men who were opening the gates to let her in
Have fallen to the ground. An owl in mid-air
Has wrenched itself upward screaming, and smashed
Down to the yard—there falls another! Oh,
Are these the flowers we throw at her feet?
You asked us for life, Moses; what life have you
Against this death which pushes through the gate
Shoulder to shoulder with the bride? Moses,
It is now that you must break through to your power,
Now! It's here.

MOSES.   The shadows are too many.
All was right, except this, all, the reason,
The purpose, the justice, except this culmination.
Good has turned against itself and become
Its own enemy. Have we to say that truth
Is only punishment? What must we say
To be free of the bewildering mesh of God?
Where is my hand to go to? Ramases,
There's no more of me than this. This is all:
I followed a light into a blindness.

TEUSRET.   Come
Away, Ramases, Ramases, come now.
You must meet her and love her.

Isn't it in love that life is strongest?
I want you to love her. Already we're late.

RAMASES. Why is she sighing, Teusret? Such great sighs.
They have taken all the air. Now there will be
Nowhere to breathe. Come with me.

[*He crumples and falls*

TEUSRET.   Ramases,
I don't know the way!

RAMASES.   I am finding it for you.
Stoop, Teusret. You see? You cannot lose me.
Here I am. [*He dies.*]

TEUSRET.   Where? Where? Ramases!
I'll meet her alone, then. When she comes she'll reach you.
She must, she must. She came so far.

[*She runs to the courtyard*

ANATH. Ramases, can you forget life so quickly?
This is my hand, a living hand, remember?
My dear, my pharaoh of sleep, you have
The one sure possession of the world.

SETI. What's that movement? The light touching his ring.
Is that all that light can do? Here are his eyes.
Play here, as you did. Why will you waste on a stone?
A stone. Stone.

MOSES.   This is how it is
To make time your friend. The earth has come and gone.
For him the earth has gone. But for us it still
Hangs in the air, like a smell of burning
Which must be searched for, so slight, but we cannot rest
Until, like this, we have put it out.

[87]

SETI [*to* MOSES].   You have done
What you returned for. You found us in the morning.
Leave us with what remains of the night. The day
You found us in is over.

ANATH. You have the freedom of the darkness, Moses.
Why do you wait? Haven't you recognized
The triumph of your purpose? Your twelve hundred
Thousand souls, out there in the dungeon of the night,
Are waiting to hear the long bolts grate back.
Ramases has died,
And the air stands ready in the wilderness to take you in.
Ramases has died. Tomorrow the lizards
Will be sparkling on the rocks. Why aren't you dancing
With such liberty for such starving souls?

MOSES. I do not know why the necessity of God
Should feed on grief; but it seems so. And to know it
Is not to grieve less, but to see grief grow big
With what has died, and in some spirit differently
Bear it back to life. The blame could impale me
For ever; I could be so sick of heart
That who asked for my life should have it; I could believe
Creation to be no more than a weight of stone
Quarried for the chisel of doom; or I could see
Man's life go forward only by guilt and guilt.
Then we should always watch Ramases dying,
Whereas he had such life his death can only
Take him for a moment, to undo his mortality,
And he is here pursuing the ends of the world.
There is a wilderness between my blood and peace.

Enter AARON

AARON. We are standing ready. The sound of the wings is quiet
And the stars are fading in silence.

[88]

All ears wait for your command to march.
Egypt is throwing away its gold to have us gone.
Is it now?

MOSES.   Now! At last the crying of our past
Is over. Anath—Egypt—
Why should it have been I that had to be
Disaster to you? I suffer victory
And my joy is armed with pain. Triumph I know;
But Egypt broken was mother of my triumph.
Now, always unknown to each other, you and I
Must force the arduous, damnable pass of time.
Farewell.

ANATH.   You have nothing now except the wilderness.

MOSES. The wilderness has wisdom.
And what does eternity bear witness to
If not at last to hope? Eternal failure
Would make creation void before the void
Had seen creation.

Re-enter TEUSRET

TEUSRET.   I have seen her. O Ramases,
Are you so taken with the dark
That what has dazzled me won't open your eyes?
Ramases, she has come so gifted for you,
With a fable of rubies, and pearls like seeds of the moon.
Doesn't their brightness come to you? Do they glimmer
Nowhere into the cupboards of your sleep?

SETI. She need bring nothing, except the hour that has gone.

MOSES. Death and life are moving to a call.
I turn from Egypt.

ANATH.   What is left
To call to me?

MOSES.   The morning, which still comes
    To Egypt as to Israel, the round of light
    Which will not wheel in vain.
    We must each find our separate meaning
    In the persuasion of our days
    Until we meet in the meaning of the world.
    Until that time.

                          [*He goes. The early light reaches* RAMASES

                  THE CURTAIN FALLS

                  THE PLAY ENDS

PRINTED IN
GREAT BRITAIN
AT THE
UNIVERSITY PRESS
OXFORD
BY
CHARLES BATEY
PRINTER
TO THE
UNIVERSITY